Diane Warner's Complete Guide to a Traditional Wedding

Everything You Need to Create Your Perfect Day:
Time-Tested Toasts, Vows, Ceremonies, and Etiquette

By Diane Warner

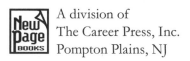

A division of
The Career Press, Inc.
Pompton Plains, NJ

392.5
War

Copyright © 2014 by Diane Warner

DIANE WARNER'S COMPLETE GUIDE TO A TRADITIONAL WEDDING
TYPESET BY DIANA GHAZZAWI
Cover design by Joanna Williams
Printed in the U.S.A.

To order this title, please call toll-free 1-800-CAREER-1 (NJ and Canada: 201-848-0310) to order using VISA or MasterCard, or for further information on books from Career Press.

The Career Press, Inc.
220 West Parkway, Unit 12
Pompton Plains, NJ 07444
www.careerpress.com
www.newpagebooks.com

Library of Congress Cataloging-in-Publication Data

Warner, Diane.
    Diane Warner's complete guide to a traditional wedding : everything you need   to create your perfect day : time-tested toasts, vows, ceremo-nies, and
etiquette / by Diane Warner. -- 1 Edition.
        pages cm
    Includes bibliographical references and index.
    ISBN 978-1-60163-297-5 (hardcover : alk. paper)
    ISBN 978-1-60163-494-8 (ebook : alk. paper)
        1. Weddings--United States--Planning. 2. Consumer education--United
States. I. Title. II. Title: Complete guide to a traditional wedding.
HQ745.W3673 2013
392.5--dc23
                                                                                        2013035452

I would like to dedicate this book to my family:
my husband, Jack;
my children, Darren, and his wife, Lisa,
and Lynn, and her husband, Ron;
and my four amazing grandchildren,
Caleb, Renee, Jeffrey, and Lyndi.

Acknowledgments

My sincere thanks to my agent, Jeff Herman, and the editorial staff at Career Press, including Adam Schwartz, Michael Pye, and Kirsten Dalley, and a special thanks to Diana Ghazzawi. Also, I would like to thank all the brides and grooms who so generously shared their stories, as well as the wedding professionals who offered their advice and expertise. Thank you, all.

Contents

Why This Book Now?

We live in an uncertain world filled with financial challenges and pressure from every side. This has caused engaged couples to return to one reassuring certainty that still exists: a traditional wedding ceremony, yet personalized with their own special touches, resulting in a day uniquely their own. Their goal is to avoid a cookie-cutter wedding with all its predictable elements by creating a one-of-a-kind masterpiece that is meaningful, poignant, and memorable.

As you read through this book, highlight ideas that appeal to you. You'll find that in addition to traditional touches, I've included the latest trends, such as including pets in your ceremony and reception, Dad's giving-away words, and destination weddings.

Enjoy the journey as you plan your special day.

Part 1

You're Engaged! Now What?

Congratulations! You're engaged! What a happy time for you!

So, let's talk about what happens next.

I recommend that both of you take a little time to dream before making any concrete plans. Don't make decisions until you have a vision of what your wedding should look like.

Close your eyes. What do you see? A vast cathedral with stained glass windows? An ivy-covered brick chapel? An outdoor wedding on a hillside overlooking a sandy beach?

Who do you want in attendance? As many guests as possible? Or a small, intimate group of close friends and family members?

What type of ceremony do you envision? Religious? Civil? Formal? Informal?

Your choices are important because they will dictate the rest of your wedding plans, including the style and length of your bridal gown, the size of your wedding party, and the quantity and type of food served at the reception.

You'll feel like you're jumping onto a moving train as you're faced with dozens of decisions and activities. You're in for quite a ride. But don't worry—it'll all be worth it when your feet touch down at your honeymoon destination. I promise.

Chapter 1

All Aboard!

Now that you're aboard, take a deep breath and get ready to plan your wedding. You can't plan everything at once, so let's take a look at your initial concerns, which are:

- Announcing your engagement.
- Setting your wedding date.
- Establishing your wedding budget.
- Creating your personal wedding Website.
- Choosing the members of your wedding party.
- Compiling your guest list.
- Establishing your gift registries.
- Setting up a prenuptial agreement, if desired.
- Creating a to-do list.

Announcing Your Engagement

Once your family members have been told about your engagement, you're ready to let the rest of the world in on your good news. The first step is to make the announcement on your favorite social networking site, through word of mouth with friends and coworkers, or at an "announcement party," which is similar to an engagement party except that it includes a surprise announcement.

A formal announcement is accomplished by submitting your information to your local newspaper. Call the newspaper to find out what advance notice they require. Society editors usually need a month to six weeks before the announcement is printed. The announcement usually includes:

- Names, hometowns, and educational backgrounds of the bride and groom.
- Names of the bride's parents, grandparents, and attendants.
- Date, time, and place of the ceremony.
- Where the couple will be honeymooning.
- Where they will reside after the honeymoon.

What the Groom Needs to Know

Although diamond rings are the most popular (75 percent of engaged women wear a diamond), other gems—for example, a ruby, sapphire, emerald, amethyst, or pearl—are equally beautiful, just as "official," and often less expensive. Even Princess Kate wore a sapphire engagement ring. Another less expensive option is to convert a family heirloom ring into an engagement ring by providing a modern setting for the stone. Or, if your bride has her heart set on a one-carat diamond ring, which isn't within your budget at the moment, purchase the same exact ring with a cubic zirconia stone instead. Then, when you're financially able, have the ring re-set with a genuine diamond—perhaps on your first wedding anniversary. This little trick is more popular than you would think. The cubic zirconia, if kept sparkling clean, will appear to be a diamond for all practical purposes. Of course, this delicious scheme will remain a secret between you and your bride—no need to breathe a word about it to *anyone*.

Setting Your Wedding Date

Religious traditions often determine the time and day of the ceremony. For example, a Jewish wedding is traditionally held after sundown on a Saturday evening, or on a Sunday; it may never be held on the Sabbath, between sundown on a Friday and sundown on a Saturday. Most Roman Catholic weddings are held between eight in the morning and noon, although that custom has been relaxed quite a bit in the past 20 years or so. Christians usually don't marry on a Sunday. One of the first things you need to do if you're planning a religious ceremony is to meet with your clergyman to clear the date and time of your wedding.

When choosing your wedding date, consider your available vacation days, and avoid a date that conflicts with special family occasions, such as a special birthday or a bar mitzvah.

Morning and afternoon weddings are usually less formal and require less elaborate food and drink. The least expensive wedding, when it comes to the reception food, is in between meals when you can serve light finger foods or simply cake and champagne. Evening weddings with formal sit-down dinners are the most expensive.

To save money, plan your wedding for a Thursday or Friday night, or a Sunday afternoon. Avoid Saturday altogether because it's the most expensive day for a wedding—specifically, Saturday at 7 p.m. Also, don't get married during May, June, or August, the most popular, and therefore the most expensive months to get married. According to the Greeting Card Association (*www.greetingcard.org*), the order of popularity for wedding months is:

1. June	7. December
2. August	8. November
3. May	9. April
4. July	10. February
5. September	11. March
6. October	12. January

Save-the-date cards

Save-the-date cards are often sent a year or more in advance to friends and family members who won't want to miss the wedding. A save-the-date card will avoid a guest booking a cruise or hosting some other event on your wedding day. These cards may be ordered from a stationer or created on Websites that allow you to customize your stationary.

Establishing Your Wedding Budget

This is one of the most difficult tasks when planning a wedding. It's important to establish a budget at the start so everyone involved knows where the money is coming from, where it will go, and how you plan to prioritize in order to stay within its parameters. By "prioritize," I mean you must decide which elements of your wedding are most important to you. Is a couture bridal gown at the top of your list of priorities? Or would you give up on that dream if it means honeymooning at an exotic location, instead of somewhere local? What about your reception? Does it need to be a seven-course plate-served meal at an upscale country club? Or can you plan a mid-morning wedding when only a light brunch buffet is required at the social hall of your church? You need a little time to sort out your priorities. The important thing is that you spend money on the elements that mean the most to you. Of course, if money isn't a factor, go for it and have the ultimate wedding of your dreams.

Traditionally, the bride's parents pay for most of the wedding expenses, while the groom's parents pay for the rehearsal dinner and a few other expenses. In today's world, however, it has become a joint venture between the bride, groom, their parents, and other relatives. In other cases, financially stable couples pay for the entire wedding themselves.

If either set of parents springs for most of the wedding expenses, this does not give them the right to *plan* the wedding. Regardless of who is paying for the wedding, this is your wedding, not your mother's and not your Aunt Bessie's. So, as kindly as possible, thank everyone for their financial contributions, but make it clear that you and your fiancé will be making the major planning decisions. If this isn't well accepted, you may need to turn down their financial help, even if it means planning a less elaborate wedding you can afford from your own funds.

Traditionally, the bride and her family pay for the:
- Family engagement party.
- Wedding gown, accessories, and trousseau.
- Cost of wedding coordinator.
- Rental of ceremony and reception sites.
- Decorations for each site.
- All flowers, except for those worn by the bride, groom, groomsmen, parents, and grandparents.
- Musicians' fees.
- Transportation of the bridesmaids to the ceremony and reception.

- Entire cost of the reception, including the food, cake, beverages, caterer's fees, and gratuities.
- All photography, videography, and the bride's engagement photograph.
- Lodging for all out-of-town bridesmaids and bride's relatives.
- Gift baskets for out-of-town guests.
- Groom's wedding ring and wedding gift from the bride to her groom.
- Services of a salon on the day of, or the day preceding your wedding day, including hairdressers, pedicurists, manicurists, and makeup artists.
- Cost of blood test, if necessary.

Traditionally, the groom and his family pay for the:

- Marriage license.
- Cost of blood test, if necessary.
- Officiant's fee.
- Rehearsal dinner/party.
- Groom's wedding attire.
- Lodging for out-of-town groomsmen and groom's relatives.
- Gift baskets for out-of-town guests.
- Gifts for the best man, groomsmen, and ushers.
- Boutonnieres for the groom, the best man, the groom's attendants, both fathers, and grandfathers.
- The bride's bouquet and going-away corsage.
- Corsages for both mothers and all grandmothers.
- The bride's wedding ring and wedding gift from the groom to his bride.
- Honeymoon.

The bride's attendants pay for:

- Their own attire.
- Transportation to and from the city where the wedding will take place.

- Shared expenses of a bridal shower and bachelorette party.
- Gifts for the bridal shower.
- Joint wedding gift.

The groom's attendants pay for:

- Their own attire.
- Transportation to and from the city where the wedding will take place.
- Shared expenses of the bachelor party.
- Joint wedding gift.

Money-Saving Tips

Here are a few sources you may have overlooked that can help fund your wedding:

- Savings bonds sitting around in your bank deposit box.
- An old vehicle, boat, or motorcycle you can sell.
- A small lot, cabin, or other real estate you may have inherited several years ago. Can it be sold quickly?
- Insurance policies with cash value.
- A family garage sale. People will buy anything!

It's a good idea to have one person in charge of the budget, including the inflow and outflow of the money, and how much money is still available in each category. Assign this task to someone who is highly organized, the type of person who enjoys balancing the checkbook and gets a kick out of doing income taxes.

Create Your Personal Wedding Website

Most engaged couples establish a wedding Website—the sooner the better. In this digital age, a wedding Website is not only convenient for your friends and family members, but it's an enormous time-saver for the bride and groom. Find a Website that will help you create your own in a streamlined way. Google "how to create a wedding Website," where you'll find dozens of sites that are free or charge a small fee. Some of these sites advertise that you can create your wedding Website in "5 minutes." Here are a few examples:

- eWedding.com
- Wix.com
- WeddingPaperDivas.com

Here are just a few things you can upload to your wedding Website:

- Engagement photo.
- Video of your wedding proposal.
- Date and locations of your ceremony and reception, including maps.
- Biographical sketches of the members of your wedding party.
- Gift registries.
- Online guest book.
- Constantly updated newsletter.
- Audio recording of the music you plan to use when you walk down the aisle.
- Information for the out-of-town guests when they arrive, including hotel reservations, maps, and directions.
- RSVP section that allows guests to RSVP online.
- Message board for live interactive discussions.
- Wedding photos once the wedding is over.

Wedding newsletter

A wedding newsletter is separate from a wedding Website, although it may be uploaded to your Website. A newsletter contains much of the same information as your wedding Website, but it is usually e-mailed, faxed, snail-mailed, or placed on your social media page. It keeps your friends and relatives up-to-date on your plans.

Choosing the Members of Your Wedding Party

The total number of attendants may be determined by the wedding's formality or by the couple's tastes. Here is a list of attendants you will need to select:

A maid or matron of honor

This woman is also known as your honor attendant or chief bridesmaid. Her duties are to help you in any way she can. She helps the bride shop for her gown, accessories, and bridesmaids' attire; plans and hosts a bridal shower; attends the bridal luncheon; helps the bride dress before the ceremony; holds the bride's bouquet during the ceremony; safeguards the groom's ring; signs the wedding certificate; and stands in the receiving line, if there is one. She also dances with the best man during the reception and helps the bride change into her going-away attire.

|||||||||||||||||||||||||||||||||||||||||||||||||||||||||||||||||||||||||||||||||||||||||||||||||||

Etiquette 101

The bride's mother may serve as her daughter's matron of honor, or the bride may have two honor attendants: a matron of honor and a maid of honor. Another option is for the bride to choose a man as her honor attendant. Likewise, the groom's father may serve as his son's best man, or the groom may choose a woman as his best woman.

|||||||||||||||||||||||||||||||||||||||||||||||||||||||||||||||||||||||||||||||||||||||||||||||||||

Best man

The best man is the groom's right-hand man in the days preceding the wedding. He is also his biggest support during the big day itself. His duties are to help the groom locate an acceptable tuxedo rental store, make arrangements for the groomsmen to be measured for their tuxes, pick up their attire on the wedding day, and confirm or pick up anything the groom has ordered, including airline tickets and honeymoon reservations. He plans the bachelor party; safeguards the bride's ring and the marriage license; signs the wedding certificate; helps decorate the couple's getaway vehicle; delivers the fee to the officiant; stands in the receiving line, if there is one; dances with the bride, her mother, and her attendants; serves as master of ceremonies during the reception (unless there is an official host); offers the first toast to the bride and groom; secures any wedding gifts brought to the reception; and returns all the men's attire. Whew!

The best man and the rest of the members of the groom's wedding party usually get involved in decorating the get-away vehicle. Also, if the wedding takes place in a small town, it's often traditional for members of the wedding party and other guests to lead a wedding parade down Main Street. Here are a few popular ways to decorate the get-away vehicle, as well as some tips:

- Attach an oversized photo of the bride and groom to the back of the car, surrounded by crepe paper flowers and ribbons. (Take a photo to your local drug store and have it blown up into a poster.)

- Tie a floral bouquet to the hood ornament of the car.

- Attach helium balloons, tissue wedding bells, pompoms, and streamers to the vehicle.

- Use a "Just Married" car kit which can be purchased from your local wedding or party supply store.

- Attach tin cans, old shoes, or novelty items denoting the couple's hobbies, such as school books wrapped tightly with a narrow belt, an old stethoscope, golf clubs, tennis rackets, etc. If the bride or groom is a Realtor, attach a sign that reads: "This One's Sold!" For the groom who is a fireman, attach a sign that reads, "Gonna Be a Three-Alarm Fire Tonight!" You get the idea.

- Don't use glue, cellophane tape, rubber cement, or regular paint of any kind.

- Keep the windshield clear. Don't write anything on it.

- If there's a chance for rain, ditch the crepe paper idea because it will "bleed" all over the car and may cause permanent stains.

Bridesmaids

The bridesmaids have relatively light duty: help the honor attendant plan and host a bridal shower; run small errands or make telephone calls; attend the bridal luncheon; stand in the receiving line, if asked; and smile and look pretty.

Don't choose your attendants based on their size, height, or attractiveness. Choose them because you love them and want them standing beside you on the most important day of your life. The attendants do *not* need to be a matched set, like carriage horses.

Groomsmen and ushers

You may have separate groomsmen and ushers, or the groomsmen may also serve as ushers before the ceremony begins. Here are their duties: help the best man with pre-wedding and post-ceremony responsibilities, such as decorate the get-away vehicle; assemble the wedding party for the photographer; usher wedding guests to their seats; hand out ceremony programs; roll out the aisle runner; hand out maps to the reception venue; dance with the bride, both mothers, and every bridesmaid; smile and look handsome.

Once you've chosen your groomsmen, commission them as special agents on your wedding day; they should constantly watch for problems or potential disasters in the making. For example, they may be able to help the caterer as he frantically searches for an extra serving table, or they may notice a guest in distress.

Flower girl(s)

A flower girl precedes the bride down the aisle, carrying a basket of flowers or tossing rose petals in the bride's path. She may walk beside the ring bearer, or, if there are two flower girls, they may walk down the aisle holding hands, or side by side as they toss their rose petals. Hopefully, she will smile and look adorable.

Whether as a flower girl, ring bearer, or other member of the wedding party, don't include children who are too young. By too young, one minister I spoke with said his policy is that a child must be at least 4 years old. Other wedding professionals recommend children be no younger than 5 years old. Seat a parent or relative of a young flower girl or ring bearer at the end of an aisle near the front of the ceremony venue so that, if one of the cuties gets a little *too* cute up there, that person can discretely escort the child back to sit with the family.

Ring bearer

The ring bearer precedes, or accompanies, the flower girl down the aisle. If there is no flower girl, he precedes the bride. He carries an elegant white or velvet pillow, or a silver tray that has the bride's "ring" attached with a satin ribbon. Of course, this is just for show, because the real ring is being safeguarded by the best man. *Never* let the ring bearer carry the actual ring. If you choose to have two ring bearers, the two boys walk side by side down the aisle, and the second ring bearer carries the groom's "ring."

Train bearers or pages

If you have several boys and girls vying for the positions of flower girl and ring bearer, and your wedding gown happens to have a long train, these young children can serve as train bearers or pages. Their sole responsibility is to carry the train of the bridal gown during the processional and recessional.

Junior attendants

Junior attendants are usually between 8 and 15 years of age. The bride's junior attendants are called junior bridesmaids and precede the bridesmaids down the aisle. They stand at the end of the row of bridesmaids. The groom's junior attendants are called junior groomsmen or ushers and stand at the end of the row of groomsmen. This is a thoughtful way to include the bride's or groom's brothers or sisters. Don't worry if you have an uneven number of junior attendants.

Candle lighters

Candle lighters light the candles during the candlelighting prelude, which immediately precedes the seating of the bride's mother. They also snuff out the candles after the recessional.

Bell ringer(s)

Bell ringers are young boys or girls who walk up and down the aisles of the ceremony venue ringing crystal or brass bells before the ceremony begins. Traditionally, the ringing of these bells was thought to ward off evil spirits, but in today's wedding, it's simply a way to let the guests know the ceremony is about to begin. They precede the candlelighters.

Etiquette 101

If your ceremony will take place in a house of worship, check with your officiant to see if there are any religious restrictions regarding your maid/matron of honor and best man. Some faiths require that your official witnesses (your honor attendants) be members of their faith, and they may even be required to attend special pre-wedding classes before they are allowed to participate in the ceremony.

Compiling Your Guest List

Compiling your guest list is one of the most difficult, but important, tasks when it comes to controlling the cost of your wedding. When you consider that Reuters.com reports that the average per-guest cost for a wedding is $196, you'll think twice before inflating your guest list. Remember that each guest may be accompanied by a spouse, significant other, or children.

Let's assume you plan to invite the same guests to the ceremony and the reception. This means that, although the church may hold 450 people, you may only be able to afford to feed 150 at the reception. This means one of two things: limit your ceremony guest list to the same number you can afford to feed, or have two receptions: a simple reception for everyone, with finger foods and drinks, and a second reception limited to the wedding party, close friends, and family. The problem comes when those invited to the first reception find out there is a second reception—to which they aren't invited. My personal preference is the former: only invite as many ceremony guests as you can afford to feed at a one-and-only reception.

Traditional etiquette says the guest list should be divided equally between the bride's and groom's families. However, in today's real world, the guest list may be split three ways: guests of the bride's family, the groom's family, and the couple themselves. Allowances are made when one family is considerably larger than the other. For example, your list may break down like this:

Groom's family: 65 guests

Bride's family: 55 guests

Bride and groom: 50 guests

Remember, members of your wedding party are on the guest list, too.

You can create a customized guest list on your computer, purchase a guest list organizer, or keep your list on a simple legal pad. These are the components each list should contain: name, address, home or cell number, e-mail address; columns for responses to RSVPs, description of gifts received, and the dates thank-you notes are mailed. If you are making a handwritten list, watch out for misspellings when addressing the invitations, especially if someone else will be helping with this chore.

Here are some ideas to trim a guest list:

- Don't invite guests just to satisfy business obligations.

- Although a guest's spouse must be invited, a single guest's escort does not, unless the couple is engaged or in a long-term relationship.

- Limit your guest list to those 16- or 18-years-old or older. Even so, there will be small children running around, so one idea is to set up a children's table where less expensive foods are served.

- Although you must invite everyone to your wedding who was invited to a pre-wedding party (such as an engagement party, a bridal shower, or a co-ed shower), don't get caught up in the fallacy of thinking the more guests, the better chance you have to compensate for the cost of the wedding. You may only receive one gift for every two to four guests, because people usually go in on a gift together. Certainly, you can't count on cash gifts to cover your expenses. It just won't happen.

Be willing to compromise and prioritize from the very beginning of your planning. Obviously, a large, upscale, formal wedding is more expensive than a smaller, informal wedding, so you'll need to be realistic about what you can actually afford, depending on available wedding funds.

What the Groom Needs to Know

I know it's a lot less hassle just to let your bride and her mom worry about the guest list, but this is one way you can really help out. Take an interest in your guest list, make suggestions, and be as patient as you can. Unfortunately, compiling the guest list can become a little stressful, but all your wedding plans won't be this contentious, so just smile and handle it the best you can. By the way, if you're good with Excel, you'll become a hero by keeping track of the guest list RSVPs. You'll be the go-to-guy to find out how many guests have responded.

Setting Up Prenuptial Agreements

Regarding prenuptial agreements, it's never too early to discuss this possibility with your fiancé. This is a contract between you and your intended that you sign before you get married. It explains rights and benefits that will exist during the marriage and—heaven forbid!—after the marriage in case of divorce. Most couples think a pre-nup is only for the rich and famous, or for couples who were married before and have complicated financial issues. Actually, any couple can benefit from one of these contracts.

Here are some of the most important factors addressed in one of these agreements:

- After you're married, how will you take legal ownership of property owned by each of you beforehand, including real estate, stock portfolios, summer homes, and other investments?
- How will you handle business interests?
- How will you manage inheritance payments, alimony, or child support payments?
- How will assets be accumulated during your marriage—jointly or individually?
- Which one of you is responsible to pay any debts accumulated before the wedding? How about debts accumulated after the wedding?
- What will you do about life insurance provisions, pensions, IRAs, and 401K accounts?
- In case of divorce, how will your joint assets be divided?

Establishing Your Gift Registries

According to Brides.com, more than 90 percent of couples establish gift registries, and the average wedding guest spends between $70 and $100 on a wedding gift. A computerized gift registry is a wish list established at a variety of stores by the bride and groom so that friends and relatives will know what to purchase as shower or wedding gifts.

Register as soon as you become engaged. Although guests aren't required to purchase from your registries, at least they are available to them. These registries are offered by stores as a free service, along with the guidance of a professional wedding gift consultant, who will help the bride and groom make their selections.

Traditionally, the bride registers at an upscale department store for her choices of linens, china, crystal, silver, cookware, and so forth. In today's world, however, the bride and groom may register at any store for gifts such as:

- Camping and mountaineering equipment.
- Gardening tools.
- Furniture and appliances.
- Down payment on a home—register with a mortgage company.
- The honeymoon—register with a travel agency.
- Artwork for your home—register with an art gallery.

Etiquette 101

Traditionally, it has been in poor taste to list your gift registries on the bottom of your wedding invitations. However, the rules have slackened a bit to allow for a small insert card that lists your registries, but these cards should only be inserted into invitations to close friends and family members. It's still considered a no-no to include them in *all* the invitations. A tactful alternative is to include a card that gives your wedding Website. Of course, your wedding Website will contain your gift registries, where your guests will "just happen to see" them.

It's still in poor taste to ask for cash, unless your parents can get the word out discretely to very, *very* close friends or relatives.

Creating a To-Do List

The following is a to-do list that will help keep your wedding planning on track.

As soon as possible

- Choose your wedding date.
- Reserve ceremony/reception venues.

- Choose members of your wedding party.
- Decide on a theme and color scheme.
- Establish your wedding budget.
- Apply for passports, visas, or certified copies of your birth certificates, if needed, for your marriage license or out-of-country honeymoon travel.
- Arrange for the parents to meet each other, if applicable.
- If you're planning a religious ceremony, meet with your rabbi, priest, or minister.
- Establish your guest list.
- Hire your wedding coordinator, if you plan to use one.
- Begin planning the reception, including hiring vendors and service providers.
- Buy the wedding gown and accessories.
- Meet with the bridesmaids and junior bridesmaids to choose their dresses.
- The mother of the bride should purchase her dress right away so that she can show it to, or send a photo to the mother of the groom. This will give the groom's mother plenty of time to purchase a complementary dress.
- Begin researching honeymoon destinations. Pick up brochures at travel agencies and research online. It takes longer than you would think to compare locations and resorts. Also, the most popular honeymoon destinations become booked in advance, and you don't want to have to settle for a second or third choice. See Chapter 10 for suggestions.

Four to five months before the wedding
- Make final plans for your reception.
- Assemble friends and family members to make items ahead of time, such as pew bows, wedding favors, and other decorations.
- Place your order with your stationer.
- Place your catering order, including your wedding cake.
- Place your floral order.

- Book musicians for your ceremony and/or reception.

- The groom should book reservations for the honeymoon, including a bridal suite for the wedding day.

- Round up volunteers who are willing to help out the day before the wedding with such things as decorating the ceremony and reception venues, arranging fresh flowers, and so on.

Three to four months before the wedding

- Plan the details of the ceremony, including the writing of personalized vows, if desired.

- Reserve the men's formalwear rentals.

- Schedule an appointment for blood tests, if necessary.

- Have your teeth cleaned and checked.

- Begin addressing the wedding invitations.

Two to three months before the wedding

- Round up the incidentals, such as the guest book and pen, ring pillow, garter, and the "something old, something new, something borrowed, something blue, and a penny for your shoe."

- Make up a list of "must" shots for the photographer and videographer.

- Make up lists of "play" and "don't play" musical selections for your DJ or band.

- Have your salon stylist practice your wedding hairstyle and makeup.

- Write thank-you notes for all gifts received so far from bridal showers, engagement parties, or early wedding gifts.

- Apply for the marriage license, depending on the licensing rules in your state.

- Send a wedding announcement to your local newspaper.

- Attend pre-marital counseling, as required.

Four to six weeks before the wedding

- Plan the bridesmaids' luncheon and the bachelor and bachelorette parties.

- Schedule final fittings for all wedding attire.

- Wear your wedding shoes around the house for several days to break them in (unless you're using the "decorated tennies" idea in Chapter 2).
- Coordinate the wedding rehearsal and send out rehearsal invitations.
- Address wedding announcements to be mailed a day or two after the wedding. These announcements are only sent to out-of-towners who aren't invited to the wedding itself.
- Purchase or borrow luggage for your honeymoon, if necessary.
- Have final face-to-face meetings with all your vendors and service providers.
- Call all your volunteers to confirm their duties.
- Book accommodations for out-of-town guests.

Three to four weeks before the wedding
- Arrange for all the men to be measured for their wedding attire.
- Finalize details of wedding rehearsal and rehearsal dinner.
- Book transportation for the wedding party to and from the ceremony venue.

Two to three weeks before the wedding
- Confirm the RSVPs for the reception and call the caterer with the final number of guests.
- Start packing for your honeymoon.
- Arrange for paid or volunteer workers for a nursery or kiddies' room during the ceremony and/or the reception.
- Sit down with your family and your fiancé's family to determine ceremony seating for family members and special guests. This list should be given to the groomsmen or ushers who will be seating the guests before the ceremony.
- Likewise, make up a seating plan for the reception.
- Arrange for someone to transport wedding gifts to your home after the reception.

One to two weeks before the wedding

- Provide a time schedule to everyone involved in the ceremony and reception.

- The groom or wedding coordinator should contact each vendor and service provider to go over all last-minute details and time schedules.

- The groom or best man should confirm honeymoon reservations.

- Have final fittings for wedding attire.

- Attend the bridesmaids' luncheon.

- Confirm rehearsal plans with the officiant.

- Pack personal supplies that will be needed for the rehearsal, wedding, and reception.

- Attend bachelor and bachelorette parties.

- Keep appointments for hair styling, pedicures, manicures, and makeup artistry.

- *Important!* Give the marriage license to the officiant during the wedding rehearsal.

If you can accomplish the tasks discussed in this chapter as soon as possible after you become engaged and set your wedding date, you'll have a leg up on your plans.

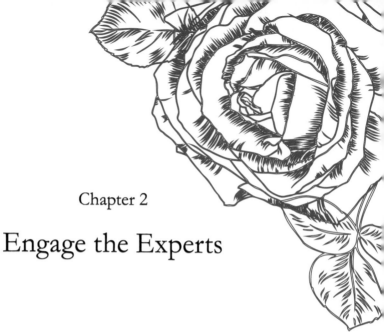

Chapter 2

Engage the Experts

Your experts include vendors and service providers who will work with you to give you the dream wedding you envision. They may include:

- Professional wedding coordinator.
- Officiant.
- Stationer.
- Ceremony venue.
- Reception venue.
- Bridal salon.
- Formalwear store.
- Caterer.
- Pastry chef/bakery.
- Florist.
- Musicians.
- Photographer.
- Videographer.
- Limousine rental company.
- Insurance agent.

A wedding show, a bridal show, or a "bridal extravaganza," as they're sometimes called, is a must for a bride and groom in the early stages of planning. These shows feature every kind of wedding vendor you'll need, except the officiant. Even if you don't hire any of them, you'll at least have an idea of how much each vendor charges.

Before hiring any vendor or service provider, call the Better Business Bureau in your city and your state's Department of Consumer Affairs to see if any of these companies have received complaints. Then talk to friends and relatives who have either hosted their own weddings, or been a guest at weddings, to glean their impressions of various bands, caterers, or other service providers. If the professionals you have in mind pass these tests, you're ready to meet with each one in person.

Professional Wedding Coordinator

There are several types of wedding coordinators, from the consultant provided by a church or synagogue for a minimal fee, to a bridal consultant who helps plan the wedding, to the full-service professional.

Full-service professionals, known as wedding coordinators, not only help plan the wedding and engage the vendors, but also supervise all the wedding activities, including the wedding rehearsal, the ceremony, and the reception. It's also possible to hire a wedding day coordinator whose sole job is to see to it that your wedding rehearsal and wedding day run smoothly, according to the plans you and your groom have made ahead of time.

A confusing factor when hiring someone to help plan your wedding is that this person may go by a variety of titles. In fact, titles seem to be interchangeable, from wedding director, to wedding professional, to wedding consultant, to wedding coordinator. The key is to find a trained, full-time professional who is a member of a professional organization, such as the Association of Bridal Consultants.

Here are some of the services a fully-trained professional will do for you:

- Helps you select your ceremony and reception sites, all your vendors (florist, caterer, musicians, photographer, videographer, etc.), all suitable to your theme, personalities, and budget.
- Ensures communication between your vendors.
- Serves as your financial advisor, counselor, etiquette expert, referee, and friend.
- Sees that your dreams come true and that your wedding rehearsal and wedding day run smoothly.

Wedding coordinators are paid in a variety of ways:

* A percentage of the wedding costs.
* Flat fees based on the services provided.
* Fees based on amount of time required.
* A small fee, plus commissions and/or referral fees from their referred vendors.

The practice of accepting commissions or referral fees is often frowned upon by professional wedding coordinators. However, if the coordinator does receive compensation from referred vendors, he is obligated to inform his client. The advantage for the bride and groom is that some of the coordinator's expenses are being paid by the vendors, which will save them money.

Before hiring a wedding coordinator, you should ask the following questions:

* Are you a certified member of a professional association?
* How long have you been in the business?
* How many weddings have you planned since you became a full-time professional?
* Can you furnish referrals?
* How do you charge?
* When is the deposit due? When are remaining payments due?
* How much time will you spend with us? Before the wedding? During the rehearsal, ceremony, and reception?

Officiant

Your choice of officiant will depend on whether you're planning a civil or religious ceremony. If you prefer a religious ceremony, you'll not only need to find a church, synagogue, or other religious venue that's available on your wedding day, but a pastor, priest, rabbi, or minister who is available as well.

If you prefer a civil ceremony, contact your local city hall or marriage license bureau to locate a county official who is legally qualified to perform the ceremony, such as a justice of the peace, judge, or county clerk. If you're planning a civil or religious ceremony at a secular venue, you'll need to find an officiant who is willing to travel to that venue.

Before engaging an officiant, you should ask:

- Are you available on the dates we have in mind for our wedding, rehearsal, and rehearsal dinner?
- Do you require premarital counseling before you agree to marry us?
- If we want a relative or another clergyman to help officiate our wedding, will he or she be allowed to do so?
- In the case of a previous divorce, are there any restrictions or requirements that must be fulfilled before you agree to marry us?
- If a religious ceremony, will we be required to commit to raising our children in the religious faith involved?
- Will we need to provide our baptism or confirmation certificates?
- Will we be allowed to write our own vows, include a unity candle ceremony, or other variations?

If the officiant requires pre-marital counseling before he or she will marry you, don't worry. This is a good thing—it can even be fun! It will bring to light differences neither one of you knew existed and give you a chance to talk about these differences before you get married. Counseling opens up communication, which will be a golden asset for both of you after the wedding.

If you're planning a civil ceremony at a secular venue, your state may issue a special temporary license to a friend or relative to perform the marriage ceremony. If this idea appeals to you, contact your county clerk's office. If so, the temporary license may be issued by a judge or the county clerk and will be valid only for a certain number of days.

Stationer

A stationer will provide you with your wedding invitations, enclosure cards, wedding announcements, thank-you notes, and ceremony programs.

The expense will be determined by the formality of your wedding—the higher degree of formality, the more expensive. Engraving is the traditional type of print technique that results in raised print that is pressed through and can be felt on the back of the paper. Thermography also results in raised print, but is not pressed through and cannot be felt on the back of the paper. Lithography imprints the lettering with ink and does not result in raised or pressed-through letters. It is a less costly option and is perfectly acceptable for wedding invitations.

You can also order online or print them yourself. Buy a wedding invitation kit that includes the invitations and the computer program you will need to compose them.

If ordering from a professional stationer, here are some helpful tips:

- Order 25 or more extra invitations, just in case you decide to invite more guests than originally planned. Also, order extra envelopes, in case you make a mistake when addressing them.

- For a formal wedding, mail your invitations six to eight weeks in advance; for an informal wedding, mail them four weeks in advance.

- Allow four to six months for the invitations to be printed.

- The invitations and enclosure cards should have the same style font.

Etiquette 101

Some things to remember when ordering your invitations include:

- It's considered poor etiquette to print "No gifts, please" on the bottom of your invitations.

- When ordering your invitations, remember this rule: when in doubt, spell it out. For example, instead of "Ave.," spell out "Avenue."

- If only one parent will be extending the invitation, replace Mr. and Mrs. John Herbert Dillon with either Mr. John Herbert Dillon or Ms. Susan Dillon.

- The language in a formal invitation differs from that of an informal one. For example, the formal "the honor of your company" is replaced with the more informal "the pleasure of your company."

- In small italicized letters at the bottom of the invitation, you may let the guests know what to expect in the way of food at the reception, with words such as "Dinner reception to follow" or "Hors d'oeuvres reception to follow."

This is a sample of wording for a formal invitation:

Mr. and Mrs. John Herbert Dillon
request the honor of your presence
at the marriage of their daughter
Ashley Marie
to
Mr. Jason Lewis Bentley
Saturday, the fifth of June
at 4 o'clock
Grace Cathedral
Maxwell, South Carolina

Here is sample wording for an invitation when the bride's parents have divorced and are remarried to someone else, but both couples want to host the wedding:

Mr. and Mrs. Donald Paul Hennington
and
Mr. and Mrs. Brent Talbot Jefferson

The following is sample wording for an invitation when the groom's parents are hosting the wedding:

Mr. and Mrs. Sean Lester Payne
request the honor of your presence
at the marriage of
Miss Dana Elise Henderson
to their son
James Harold Payne

Sample wording for a double-wedding invitation where two sisters are being married can be:

Mr. and Mrs. Jonathan Rene LeBlanc
request the honor of your presence
at the marriage of their daughters
Sherry Anne
to
Mr. Lance Robard Dixon
and
Donna Leanne
to
Mr. Victor James Hanford

Sample wording for an invitation being sent by the bride and groom may read:

The honor of your presence
is requested at the marriage of
Miss Janette Lisanne Thomas
and
Mr. Robert Dean Terrell

The following is sample wording for an informal invitation:

Two lives, two hearts
joined together in friendship
united forever in love.
It is with joy that we,
Judith Anne Larson
and
Jason Randolph Gray
invite you to share
in a celebration of love
as we exchange our marriage vows
at one-thirty in the afternoon
in the garden of
2231 Cedar Avenue
Dallas, Texas

Enclosure cards

Enclosure cards are inserted inside the wedding invitations. These may include:

- Pew card, also known as a "within the ribbon" card, which reserves a seat in a specific row which the usher will use to guide a guest to the correct pew. These designated pews are usually decorated with ribbons and flowers.

- An at-home card gives the bride's new address after she's married.

- The response card is the most common enclosure (also known as an RSVP card), which the invitees are requested to fill out and return, indicating whether they will attend the wedding or reception. Always add postage to the response cards. By the way, many brides use pencil to lightly number the backs of response cards, with the numbers corresponding to their master list of invitations. That way, if a response card is returned with the name missing, she can match it up with the number on the master list.

- An admission card is only required when the wedding ceremony is held in a venue that attracts sightseers. The guest is to present the admission card at the entrance to the facility. The card may say, *"Please present this card at St. John's Cathedral for admittance."*

- A reception card is inserted only into the invitations of those guests invited to the reception following the ceremony. It may read:

Dinner Reception
to be held following the ceremony
in the Rose Garden Room
Hilton Hotel
881 North Point Avenue

or

Cocktail Reception
immediately following ceremony
Riverside View Restaurant
Number 1 River Road

- A parking card ensures that wedding guests should never be expected to pay for parking when attending your ceremony or reception. Make arrangements with the parking garages near your venues to pick up the tab for any guest parking fees (furnish the attendants with a copy of the parking card for identification). The parking card may read:

For free parking, present this card to the attendant
when you exit the Collierville parking garage
located at 2110 Collierville Avenue

- A map card gives directions to the ceremony and/or the reception sites.

- A rain card gives the alternate location for the wedding and/or reception in case of rain. It may read: "In case of rain, the wedding and reception will be held in the Community Center, 2770 East Main Street."

- A gift registry card lists the various places where the bride and groom have registered for gifts.

||||||||||||||||||||||||||||||||||||||||||||||||||||||||||||||||||||||||||||||||||||||||||||||||||||||

Etiquette 101

If a military wedding, rank determines how an invitation is worded. Unless the bride's or groom's rank is sergeant or higher, the rank is omitted entirely, with only the mention of the branch of service. If either is a junior officer, the bride's or groom's rank is given on the line below the name. If higher than lieutenant, the title is placed in front of the name. Examples:

- Below sergeant: John Ellis MacRae, United States Army
- Junior officer: John Ellis MacRae, First Lieutenant, United States Army
- Higher than Lt: Captain John Ellis MacRae, United States Army

||||||||||||||||||||||||||||||||||||||||||||||||||||||||||||||||||||||||||||||||||||||||||||||||||||||

Post-wedding announcements

The person(s) announcing the wedding should be the same names as on the wedding invitations. Post-wedding announcements are mailed two days after the wedding. Announcements are never sent to anyone invited to the ceremony or reception. They can be worded as follows:

Mr. and Mrs. Kent Sherman Livingston
proudly announce
the marriage of their daughter
Sylvia Elise
and
Mr. Jason Everly Johnson
Saturday, the nineteenth of November
two thousand fifteen
Bellingham Community Church
Benson, Oregon

Thank-you notes

When you place your order with the stationer for your invitations, order personalized thank-you stationery at the same time. By personalized, I don't mean that your expression of thanks within the thank-you note or letter should be printed, because that is never acceptable. Personalizing does mean having your name or monogram engraved on the front or top of the stationery.

Thank-you notes sent by the bride before the wedding should be personalized differently than those sent by the bride and groom together after the wedding.

Thank-you notes sent before the wedding should have the bride's monogram (fancy initials) engraved on the front of the notes, in this order: The initial of her surname should be in large font in the center of the monogram, the initial of her first name in smaller font on the left, and the initial of her middle name on the right. The return address on the back flap of the envelope should be her home address.

Thank-you notes sent by the bride and groom after the wedding should have the couple's monogram engraved on the front of the notes, in this order: The initial of the couple's surname should be in large font in the center of the monogram. The initial of the bride's first name in smaller font on the left, and the initial of the groom's first name on the right. The return address on the back flap of the envelope should be their new home address.

See Chapter 11 for wording of thank-you notes.

Ceremony programs

In the past, traditional etiquette frowned on ceremony programs, but I think they are perfectly acceptable for today's weddings because they add a personal touch. Here are a few reasons why wedding guests enjoy reading a ceremony program:

- It introduces members of the wedding party and their relationship to the bride or groom, including interesting photos, such as the bride and her maid of honor together when they were children.

- It provides the order of the service.

- It explains any unusual or creative facets of the ceremony. For example, the fact that a standing wreath of pink roses and baby's breath is in honor of a recently deceased family member; or the fact that the bride is wearing her mother's or grandmothers' wedding gown or veil.

- It provides a way for the bride and groom to thank those who helped with the wedding.

- It becomes a treasured memento of the ceremony, not only for the bride, groom, and their families, but for the wedding guests, as well.

A ceremony program can include the following:

Page One

Rachel and Joshua
November 10, 2014
Lakewood Community Church
Lakewood, Colorado

Page Two

Parents of the Bride and Groom:
Mr. and Mrs. Charles Emerson Thompson
and
Dr. and Mrs. Arden Frances Nelson

Members of the Wedding Party

Maid of Honor
Deanna Thompson, Sister of the Bride

Best Man
Arnold Nelson, Brother of the Groom

Bridesmaids
Jill Johnson, Friend of the Bride
Helen Nelson, Sister of the Groom
Ashley Nelson, Sister of the Groom
Loni Halani, Friend of the Bride

Groomsmen
Randy Jefferson, Friend of the Groom
Gerald Nelson, Brother of the Groom
James Thompson, Brother-in-law of the Groom
John Blake, Friend of the Groom

Flower Girls
Madison Thompson, Niece of the Bride
Michelle Thompson, Niece of the Bride

Ring Bearer
Jaime Nelson, Nephew of the Groom

Candle Lighters
Darla Castro, Friend of the Bride
Linda Trump, Friend of the Bride and Groom

Officiants
Dr. Mitch Barton, Senior Pastor of Lakewood Community Church
Rev. Eugene Johns, Uncle of the Bride

Organist
Rosalie Myers, Friend of the Bride

Soloist
Patrick Washington, Friend of the Groom

Flautist
Laura Tipton, Friend of the Bride

Page Three
Order of Service

Prelude: "To God Be the Glory," performed by Laura Tipton
Candlelighting: "Jesu, Joy of Man's Desiring"
Seating of Honored Guests: "The Wedding Song," sung by Patrick Washington
Lighting of the Memorial Candle and Seating of the Mother of the Bride
Processional: "Trumpet Voluntary"
Giving of the Bride
Prayer
Scripture Reading
Pastoral Comments

Exchanging of Vows and Rings
Lighting of Unity Candle
Pronouncement of Marriage
Introduction of Bride and Groom
Jumping the Broom
Recessional: "Wedding March" from The Sound of Music
Reception to follow in Lavinda Rose Garden

Page Four

The Memorial Candle is in loving
memory of Naomi Chambers,
grandmother of the bride.
The Unity Candle symbolizes the unity
of the bride and groom as they
leave their families and become one.
The Jumping of the Broom is an African-American
wedding tradition that demonstrates the sweeping
away of the old life, and the beginning of a new life
of commitment to each other.

Special Thanks

The Classic Car Club of Lakewood for providing and decorating the getaway car!
Susan Heston, for her loving efforts coordinating our wedding.

Addressing your invitations

When addressing your wedding invitations, here are rules to follow:

- Address your invitations by hand using blue or black ink. Be sure both envelopes (outer and inner) are in the same handwriting. If you're planning an ultraformal or formal wedding, you may decide to hire a professional calligrapher to address your envelopes.

- Do not seal the invitation and then address the outer envelope because the pressure of the pen can leave an imprint on the inner envelope.

- Never use stick-on return address labels.

- The invitations and the enclosure cards should be printed in the same font.

- Don't address an invitation to someone "and guest" or "and family." If you invite a single woman, and you want to include her boyfriend, call her to get his name so that it may be included, written out in full, on the inner and outer envelopes.

- Inner envelopes are addressed with the titles and last names, or using their first and last names, such as "Mr. and Mrs. Parsons" or "George and Judy Parsons."

- Outer envelopes are addressed with all the streets, cities, and states written out entirely with no abbreviations: 1774 North Arlington Boulevard, Arlington, Texas.

- To assemble the invitations, insert the enclosure cards, place each invitation face up inside the inner envelope, insert the inner envelope inside the outer envelope with the written names on the inner envelope facing the back of the outer envelope, seal the outer envelope, and weigh for proper postage before mailing.

- It is no longer necessary to include tissue inserts. This old tradition was a necessity in the days when ink smeared.

- Mail all the invitations at once on the same day. Do not mail them as they are addressed.

- When you place your order with your stationer, take the envelopes home with you or ask to have the envelopes delivered to you as soon as possible. That way, you can start addressing them before the invitations are printed.

- Even though it may seem more convenient to hand-deliver invitations, especially to neighbors, close friends, or coworkers, wedding invitations must always be mailed directly to the homes of the invited guests.

Other printed items

Other items you may want to have printed in advance include:

- Reception menu. If you're planning a very formal reception, you may want to have your menu printed on parchment or other fine quality paper. Place one copy per table, displayed on the table beside the centerpiece, or one at each place setting if it's a sit-down dinner.

- Itineraries for out-of-town guests. It's a nice touch to provide printed itineraries for your out-of-town guests. Once they arrive in town, many of whom may be staying at the same hotel, it's a thoughtful touch to furnish them with itineraries for all the wedding happenings that will be taking place, plus interesting places they may want to visit, maps with directions to the ceremony and reception, and a timetable for activities. Here is an example of an invitation to a specially planned event:

Welcome Brunch

Friday, May 15th at 11 a.m.

at the home of James and Esther Cunningham

201 West Palmdale Drive

Transportation will be provided from

your hotel by chartered cable car.

Ceremony Venue

Your choice of ceremony site will depend on several factors. Do you want a civil or religious ceremony? How formal will your wedding be? If you decide on a religious ceremony, will you be required to be married in a house of worship, or will your clergyman, rabbi, priest, or officiant conduct the ceremony at a secular site? If the ceremony will be a civil one, will the county officiant agree to marry you at a site of your choosing?

Popular religious and civil ceremony venues include:

- Church, synagogue, temple, or other house of worship.
- Country club.
- Hotel or resort.
- Public or private garden.
- Beside a river, lake, or waterfall.
- Seashore.
- Community clubhouse.

- Elk's hall or similar.
- Country inn.
- Rented tent.
- National, state, or city park.
- Houseboat.
- Museum.
- Senior center.
- Historical venue.
- Mansion.
- Marina.
- Private wedding chapel.
- Yacht.
- Arboretum.

Before booking your ceremony venue, be sure to ask:

- Can we be married in a house of worship if we are not members of the congregation? If not, can a member sponsor us?
- How many guests will the facility seat?
- What fees are involved, and do they vary according to the day of the week?
- How many hours will we have access to the site?
- Is there any equipment available and are fees involved? (Kneeling bench, aisle runner, white chairs, and so on.)
- What services are available, such as church organist, sound system, or site wedding coordinator?
- Are there restrictions such as no applause, no contemporary music, no lighted candles, or no flash cameras allowed? Will we be allowed to attach ribbons, floral arrangements, or candelabras to the pews?
- Are there restrictions regarding wedding attire, such as yarmulkes must be worn, or no bare shoulders allowed?
- Are there other weddings or events planned the day before, the day of, or the day after the wedding?

- Are dressing rooms available?
- Will there be any existing décor available for us to use, such as Easter lilies, Christmas poinsettias, or wedding flowers from another wedding being held the same day?

Reception Venue

Your reception venue may be near or on the same premises at your ceremony site, which is ideal. Otherwise, the wedding party and guests will need to be transported to the reception site. For possible reception locations, contact your local Chamber of Commerce and historical society for sites available in your area. Also, check online for local venues.

Popular wedding reception venues include:

- Country club.
- Hotel/resort.
- Historical site, such as a museum.
- Bed and breakfast.
- Botanical garden.
- Community clubhouse.
- Elk's hall.
- Military club facility.
- National or state park facility.
- Private estate or mansion.
- Private home.
- Private or public garden.
- Public beach.
- Restaurant.
- Senior center.
- Social hall provided at the ceremony venue.
- University or college facility.
- Winery.
- Yacht.

- Rented tent. If you decide to rent a tent, be sure you also rent a floor for the tent, unless you have an existing concrete slab or tennis court that can be used.

- Novelty site, depending on your wedding's theme, such as a zoo, amusement park, ski lodge, apartment-building rooftop, or houseboat.

Have your ceremony venue serve double-duty as your reception venue. This is becoming a money-saving trend. It's called "turning of the room." After you are married, the guests are ushered outdoors or onto a deck for cocktails and hors d'oeuvres while the ceremony venue is being "turned." The "turning" may involve:

- Moving the chairs.

- Uncovering the bride's table, which has been set up in advance.

- Uncovering plates, silverware, and napkins to be used by the guests for the buffet style meal, also set up in advance.

- Rolling in food stations, each filled with a different buffet-style food dish.

- Rolling in the cake table, including plates and silverware for serving.

An alternative is to have your guests already seated at the reception tables for the ceremony. That way, the tables are already in place, complete with centerpieces. After the wedding ceremony, the guests may remain seated while the wait staff serves individual salads to each guest. Then, while the guests are eating their salads, the buffet food is rolled in or placed on existing serving tables. Also, the guests are preoccupied with the meal and may not notice how long you spend being photographed.

Etiquette 101

Don't crowd your guests during the reception. Be sure the reception venue provides enough square feet per guest:

- 12 to 14 square feet per guest for a served meal, plus a dance floor.

- 8 to 10 square feet per guest for cocktails or hors d'oeuvres reception, plus a dance floor.

Before booking the venue, be sure to ask and consider the following:

- Is the reception venue close to your ceremony site?
- Does it provide an ambience that's complementary to the style, formality, and theme of your wedding?
- Is it affordable?
- Is it large enough? What is the maximum number of people allowed?
- May alcohol be served on the premises?
- Does the facility provide liability insurance?
- Is there adequate electrical power?
- How large are the restroom facilities?
- Is security staff provided?
- If an open-air facility, can an alternative facility be provided in case of inclement weather?
- Is cleanup included in the fee?
- Are there any musical restrictions?
- Are there any available musical instruments, such as piano or organ?
- What equipment is available, such as tables, chairs, linens, table skirts, kitchen, serving dishes, microphone, sound system, etc.?
- How many hours will the facility be available?
- Is there adequate parking and/or valet parking?
- Will there be other events taking place the same day?
- Will we be allowed to bring in our own caterer, musicians, servers, wedding cake, etc.? Or will we be required to order off their wedding menu and hire their servers, bartenders, musicians, and so forth?
- How much deposit is required? When is the balance due?
- What is the cancelation/refund policy?
- How many waiters or waitresses will be provided? (For a formal sit-down meal, they should provide one or two per 12 guests; for a buffet meal, one per 25 guests.)

What the Groom Needs to Know

Think up ways to ease the stress your bride is feeling as the big day approaches: buy her an afternoon at a spa; plan special times together, such as an all day getaway; treat her to dinner and theater tickets; or plan an evening at a concert. Or, if you both enjoy a round of golf or a day surfing at the beach, go for it! Your goal should be to break the stress cycle with a little rest and relaxation.

You can also be a great help by calling the vendors and service providers a few days before the wedding to confirm contract details, such as:

- "Exactly when will the cake be delivered to the reception venue? What is the name and phone number of the person making the delivery?"

- "Let's go over our contract one last time. Please confirm what you will be furnishing in the way of food, service, and cleanup, and the exact time you will arrive at the reception venue."

- "Let's confirm our contract. When will you arrive? How many musicians will you provide? How many hours will you play? How many breaks will you take, and how long are they?"

You should have each contract in front of you when you make the calls, and be as exact and detailed as possible as you confirm each vendor and service provider.

Book one venue to serve as your ceremony and reception venue. This is what our son and daughter-in-law did when they were married at the Lodge at Pebble Beach in Carmel, California. They booked a lovely room that opened onto a large covered veranda overlooking the 18th green. The Lodge provided chairs for the veranda ceremony, after which the guests flowed back inside where the reception took place. By the way, not only did they save money by using one venue for their ceremony and reception, but they saved an enormous amount of money by having an out-of-town wedding. Our son was a lawyer with a large law firm in Sacramento, and our daughter-in-law was a teacher at a Montessori school in Sacramento. If they would have planned a Sacramento wedding, they felt obligated to invite all their coworkers, plus friends and family. By planning an out-of-town wedding for only closest friends and relatives, they had money left over for a nicer honeymoon in Hawaii.

There are other ways to save money that would be spent at your ceremony or reception venues. Generally, outdoor venues for your ceremony and reception are less expensive than indoor venues. One option is to get married at your county courthouse, surrounded by only a few family members and close friends. Then, immediately travel to your large wedding reception, where the rest of your friends and family will be in attendance. Finally, get married at a surprise wedding that takes place during a family get-together, such as Thanksgiving, Christmas, 4th of July picnic, New Year's Eve party, or a family reunion. (Of course, your parents and the officiant aren't surprised. Everyone else will be blown away.)

Bridal Salon

A bridal salon is where you'll probably purchase the bridal attire and accessories. The female members of the wedding party may also purchase or rent their attire from the same salon. The formality of the gowns will be determined by the formality, theme, and time of day of the ceremony.

Bridal gown and accessories

The bride's gown is not only the most important purchase, but should be purchased before the bridesmaids' attire is purchased or rented. Here are general guidelines for the bridal gown, according to each degree of formality:

Ultraformal evening wedding

- Floor-length gown with embellishments, such as beading, embroidery, or lace overlay.
- The gown may have long or short sleeves; however, if short sleeved, the bride should wear elbow-length gloves.
- Her gown's train and veil should be floor length or longer.

Ultraformal daytime wedding

- Floor-length gown, but less elaborate than for an evening wedding.
- The gown may have long or short sleeves; however, if short sleeved, the bride should wear elbow-length gloves.
- The gown's train and veil may be shorter than for an evening wedding.

Formal evening wedding

- Cathedral or chapel-length gown.
- Chapel- or sweep-length train and veil.
- If the gown is short sleeved, the bride should wear elbow-length gloves.

Formal daytime wedding

- The same cathedral or chapel-length gown as required for a formal evening wedding.
- Chapel or sweep-length train and veil, or an elaborate ankle-length gown.
- If the gown has a floor-length train, it may be detachable.

Semiformal evening wedding

- Floor-length gown with no train, or ankle-length gown in white, ivory, or pastel.
- Veil is elbow-length or shorter.

Semiformal daytime wedding

- Same requirements as a semiformal evening wedding, except that the veil should be shorter.
- A bridal headpiece with a blusher veil is acceptable.

Informal daytime or evening wedding

- Cocktail length dress, a suit, or street-length dress.
- Usually, no veil, although the cocktail dress allows for a short birdcage or blusher veil attached to flowers on a simple headband, a hat, or simply flowers in the hair.

Casual wedding

Depending on the wedding's theme, the bride may wear anything she likes. For example, she might wear jeans, boots, and a western shirt for a country-western wedding, or a sarong and sandals for a Polynesian wedding.

||||||||||||||||||||||||||||||||||||||||||||||||||||||||||||||||||||||||||||||||||||||||||||||||||||||

Etiquette 101

During the ring vows, the bride's glove on her ring hand may be removed for the placement of the wedding ring, or the ring finger on the glove may be cut so that it can be easily removed during the ring ceremony. A third option, and this is my favorite, is to wear finger-less gloves.

||||||||||||||||||||||||||||||||||||||||||||||||||||||||||||||||||||||||||||||||||||||||||||||||||||||

Popular styles of wedding gown

Wedding gowns come in many shapes and styles. Here are the most popular:

- Ball gown: An extremely full skirt drops to the floor from the bride's natural waistline.
- Empire gown: The skirt drops from just under the bust line.
- Mermaid gown: Tight-fitting bodice hugs the body all the way down to the knees where a full trumpet skirt flares outward.
- Sheath gown: The fabric in this gown drops from top to bottom in one slender, unbroken line.

Popular veil styles

Likewise, there several veils to suit your gown. A simple gown can handle an elaborate veil; an elaborate gown requires a less elaborate veil. Some of the most common include:

- Ballerina length: Drops almost to the floor.
- Blusher length: Short veil that just covers the bride's face.
- Birdcage veil: A very short veil that covers part of the bride's face. (In Canada, it is known as a fascinator.)
- Cascade length: Two or more layers of different lengths.
- Cathedral length: Eight to 11 feet long, or longer.
- Chapel length: Five to eight feet long.
- Elbow length: A blusher-style veil that drops to your elbows.
- Mantilla: A long, circular piece of lace or tulle that frames the face.

Train lengths

Trains come in different lengths, including:

- Sweep length (also known as brush length): Brushes the floor or the tops of your shoes.
- Chapel length: Extends four feet from the waist.
- Cathedral length: Extends nine feet from the waist, which may require train bearers or pages to carry it when you walk down the aisle.

|||||||||||||||||||||||||||||||||||||||||||||||||||||||||||||||||||||||||||||||||||||||||||||||||||||||||||||

Etiquette 101

Some religions require that the bride wear a face veil, so if you plan to be married in a house of worship, ask the officiant before purchasing your veil or choosing an alternative headpiece.

|||||||||||||||||||||||||||||||||||||||||||||||||||||||||||||||||||||||||||||||||||||||||||||||||||||||||||||

Most brides follow the tradition of wearing "something old, something new, something borrowed, something blue, and a lucky penny in your shoe." Something old may be your grandma's hanky; something new may be your bridal gown; something borrowed may be a bracelet belonging to your best friend; something blue is usually a blue garter; and, of course, the lucky penny is worn in your shoe. The bride's accessories, including such things as her headpiece and veil, gloves, jewelry, shoes, and undergarments, may be purchased from a bridal salon, or purchased elsewhere. It has become fashionable for the affluent bride to purchase two gowns: one for the ceremony and one for the reception.

Bridesmaids and honor attendants

Their gowns should complement the bride's gown in formality, with this one caveat: they should never be longer than the bridal gown. The maid or matron of honor's gown is usually slightly different and more elaborate than the bridesmaids' gowns so that she stands out as the honor attendant. If the bride's honor attendant is a man, his attire should be the same as the groom's best man. The bridesmaids will also be required to purchase accessories, such as shoes, gloves, hat, or headpiece.

|||||||||||||||||||||||||||||||||||||||||||||||||||||||||||||||||||||||||||||||||||||||||||||||||||||

Etiquette 101

The bride must be sensitive to the differences in her brides-maids' figures. A gown won't necessarily flatter every woman. For example, one gown may flatter a small-breasted woman, but cause a well-endowed woman to "fall out" of her dress. So, choose a style that flatters all your attendants, even if you must select different style gowns for each woman. As long as the color and texture of the fabric is the same, they will look uniform. Companies such as David's Bridal offer mix and match two-piece dresses in a variety of styles and colors.

|||||||||||||||||||||||||||||||||||||||||||||||||||||||||||||||||||||||||||||||||||||||||||||||||||||

Junior bridesmaids

For a formal wedding, the junior bridesmaids' attire will be more youthful versions of the bridesmaids' gowns. For an informal wedding, they may wear a nice dress in any color complementary to those worn by the bridesmaids.

Flower girl

For a formal wedding, the flower girl may wear a white organza pinafore over a pastel, print, or velvet dress, with opaque or lace tights, and patent leather shoes or ballet slippers. Or, she may wear a custom-designed copy of the bride's or bridesmaids' gowns. Alternatively, her dress may be personalized for the wedding by adding a wide sash in the same color as the bridesmaids' gowns.

Candle Lighters

Candle lighters may be boys or girls. If girls, they may wear dresses similar or complementary to those worn by the bridesmaids or junior bridesmaids. If boys, they may wear attire similar to the groomsmen, junior groomsmen, or ushers.

Bride's and groom's mothers

The mothers' gowns or dresses should never be longer or more formal than the bride's gown, and they should be complementary to the bridesmaids' attire. Each mother should wear her own unique choice and style. An elegant suit is also a wise choice, with a hat optional for an ultraformal or formal wedding.

The bride's mother is obligated to choose her dress first, then furnish the groom's mother with a photo or drawing so she may select something complementary in color. She should make her purchase as soon as possible to give the groom's mother plenty of time to shop.

Two caveats for the mothers: don't wear white, because it may compete with the bride's gown, and don't wear anything provocative. For example, don't wear a mini-skirt or a dress that is low-cut or backless.

Men's Formalwear Store

The men's formalwear market has progressed to the point where there are dozens of styles from which to choose. Before you go into a formalwear store to select your attire, stop by one day and pick up a few of their brochures to take home with you. Also, go online and check out the many options. This will give you time to consider the different styles before making your commitment.

Once the bride and groom have a general idea of what they're looking for, they, along with their wedding coordinator, if they have one, should visit the formalwear store for a consultation. Once the store's consultant gathers all the facts, he'll be able to present various options, depending on the style and formality of the wedding, plus the wedding colors (bridesmaids' gowns, flowers, ribbon, and so forth).

Most formalwear stores offer free tuxedo rental to the groom if all the groomsmen order their tuxedos from the same store. The men will also need to rent accessories, such as ties, cufflinks, studs, and shoes.

You and your groomsmen should pick up your attire from the formalwear store two days before the wedding. This allows time to handle any mini-crises, such as the alterations weren't done yet, or the shoes you reserved are the wrong size, and so on. Don't walk into the store and blindly pick up your tux and accessories; try on *everything* there at the formalwear store. Be sure you have all the accessories and learn how to tie your bow tie properly. Be sure everything fits correctly. A common mistake is to try on the attire just prior to the ceremony, when you realize the trousers for one of your groomsmen is three inches too long.

Ultraformal evening wedding

- Tailcoats with matching trousers.
- Wing-collared shirt with white bow tie.
- White waistcoat.
- White gloves and black top hat are optional.

Ultraformal daytime wedding

- Cutaway coat with grey striped trousers.
- Wing-collared shirt with ascot or striped tie.
- Grey waistcoat.
- Grey gloves and black top hat are optional.

Formal evening wedding

- Tuxedo or white dinner jacket with complementary trousers, depending on the season.
- Dress shirt and bow tie.
- Vest or cummerbund.

Formal daytime wedding

- Grey stroller with striped trousers.
- Wing-collared shirt with striped tie, or for summer, a white suit with dress shirt, bow tie, vest, or cummerbund.

Semiformal or informal evening wedding

- Dark suit with white or colored shirt and four-in-hand tie.
- Dinner jacket with matching trousers, dress shirt, bow tie, vest, or cummerbund.
- Navy blazer with white or grey slacks, depending on the season, with dress shirt and four-in-hand tie.

Casual wedding

Wear something that complements your bride's attire, such as white slacks and a Hawaiian shirt for a Polynesian wedding.

Groom's attendants

The best man's attire is usually the same as the groom's, which distinguishes him from the groomsmen whose attire may be slightly less elaborate. For example, the groom and best man may wear vests that differ from the groomsmen and ushers. The most important thing is for the men to have a uniform appearance. If the groom has a best woman, she may wear the same attire described earlier in this chapter for the bride's honor attendant.

All the men should have a uniform appearance with consistent tailoring. Here are the guidelines:

- The tuxedo jackets should fit snugly, but with no arm bulges. There should be a little room at the waist.

- Sleeves should end at the men's wrist bones.

- Trousers should touch the top of the shoes with enough slack so the crease breaks slightly.

- The shirt collar should be tight enough to hug the neck, but not so tight that the lapels buckle. Ask your rental store for a supply of collar extenders; they're great to have on hand at the last minute.

Money-Saving Tips

The bridal gown, the bridesmaids' gowns, and the mothers' gowns may all be rented instead of purchased. The bride will probably want to purchase her own wedding veil to keep for posterity, but she can save the memory of her gown in the wedding photos and videos. The money saved will pay for twice the honeymoon you originally thought you could afford. Check the Yellow Pages or do an online search for bridal attire or wedding rentals.

Additionally, the bride can save hundreds of dollars by purchasing a white bridesmaid's gown and adding a train, if necessary, although some bridesmaids' gowns already have a train. You'll need to pursue this idea on your own because the bridal shop staff won't suggest it as an alternative.

Purchase the bride's gown from a discount outlet or Website. For example, the Gunne Sax factory in San Francisco has a separate building just for the sale of discounted wedding attire. David's Bridal also offers deep discounts on their bridal attire from time to time—you need to watch for sales. If you live near Brooklyn, New York, visit Kleinfeld's on 82nd Street, or if you live in the Boston area, visit Filene's Basement for sales. You can also purchase from a resale or consignment store that sells bridal gowns. Of course, you won't find yourself in a "Say Yes to the Dress" environment, but you might just find the perfect gown for you. Here's an unusual idea: If you live near Mexico or Canada, check out the bridal gown prices. You may save hundreds, depending on the exchange rate.

A popular trend is to shun the bridal salons for an upscale department store where the bridesmaids may find their dresses on the spot, without having to order them. If you like this idea, look for a rack filled with the exact same dress or gown in several sizes. Often bridal attendants find dresses they are more likely to wear again, and at less cost. Moreover, buy the bride's and bridesmaids' shoes from an online discount shoe store, or from Payless, Kmart, or Target. Remember, the shoes don't need to be super high quality—they only need to last for one day.

It has become trendy for the bride to decorate a pair of her comfortable, broken-in, white tennis shoes to wear on her wedding day. (This only works with a floor-length gown, however.) Decorate the tennies with white lace, beads, sequins, appliquéd lace, satin rosettes, and ribbons. Talk about a photo opp! It's also become trendy for the groom and his groomsmen to wear black tennis shoes with wide white laces.

Depending on the wedding's formality, all the men may wear their own dark suits instead of renting tuxedos. If one or two of the groomsmen don't own a dark suit, maybe they can borrow a suit from Dad, a brother, or some other friend or relative. Another option, especially for an informal afternoon wedding, is for the men to wear khaki trousers and navy blazers. Many men have this combo in their closets. The third option is to rent identical suits instead of tuxedos. This is not a huge money-saver, but it can help cut costs.

Junior groomsmen

The junior groomsmen's attire may be a younger version of the grooms-men's or usher's attire.

Ring bearer or train bearer

The ring bearer or train bearer may wear a child's version of the grooms-men's or junior groomsmen's attire.

Bride's and groom's fathers

The bride's father should follow the lead set by the groomsmen, wearing the same or similar attire. The groom's father may do likewise or wear a dark suit.

Formalwear terms

Here are some terms you should be familiar with when choosing men's attire for a wedding:

- Morning coat: Also known as a "cutaway coat." A morning coat is a must for ultraformal weddings. This coat has a broad tail and is worn with ascot and striped trousers. Added accessories include gloves and top hat.

- Dinner jacket: This jacket is white or off-white and is a preferable alternative to a dark tuxedo for warm summer months.

- Tuxedo: Usually black or gray, a tuxedo is worn with matching trousers, plus bow tie and vest or cummerbund.

- Waistcoat or vest: This is a vest that covers the trouser waistband, hence called a "waistcoat." It may match the color of the jacket or coordinate with the color of the bridesmaids' gowns.

- Four-in-hand tie: Sounds complicated, but it's actually a normal tie that men are used to wearing, but in an elegant fabric.

- Bow tie: A bow tie comes in two types: pre-tied, which is easiest to deal with, or a tie that must be hand-tied.

- Ascot: A neck scarf secured with a stick pin.

- Cummerbund: A pleated sash worn around the waist that usually coordinates with the bow tie or the color of the bridesmaids' gowns.

Many grooms decide to purchase their own tuxedo, to have in their closets when the need arises in the future. If you decide to consider this, be sure it is classic black and single-breasted that won't tend to go out of style.

Spa or Hair Salon

The bride, her attendants, and the mothers should schedule appointments the day before, or the morning of, the wedding. Be sure there will be plenty of staff on hand to take care of all of you at once. You'll want your hair styled, of course, plus optional manicures, pedicures, and facials. If your salon provides a makeup artist, arrange to go in a week or so before the wedding to have your makeup applied. That way, if you're not pleased with your makeup, you have time to experiment with it before the wedding. Some spas will provide hair stylists and makeup artists who will come to your home or venue the morning of the wedding.

Caterer

Excellent caterers have excellent reputations, so talk to friends and other brides for referrals. The time of your wedding will dictate the cost of your catered food. Obviously, a morning or afternoon requires less expensive reception food. Here are the guidelines.

Morning wedding, before 11 a.m. Continental breakfast or breakfast buffet.

Midday wedding, 11 a.m. to 1 p.m. Luncheon buffet.

Afternoon wedding, 1 to 4 p.m. Hors d'oeuvres buffet or cake and champagne only.

Early evening wedding, 4 to 7 p.m. Sit-down dinner or dinner buffet.

Ask these questions before you hire your caterer:

- How do you charge? Per plate or per food item?
- How much food will be provided per guest? (Get the specifics, such as ounces of chicken per person.)
- How will the food be served? Plate service? Sit down? Buffet table? Food stations?
- May we sample the foods before we place our order?

- May we see photos or videos of past weddings that demonstrate your food presentation?

- Do you charge a fee for cutting the cake? Per piece? Flat fee?

- Do you offer less-expensive menus for the children and service providers?

- May we see the actual linens, plates, glassware, tableware, and so forth, that you will furnish?

- Will tables be skirted? (A paper or fabric skirt that wraps the table from tabletop to floor.)

- What type of beverages will you serve? If we provide the wine or champagne, will you charge a corkage fee?

- How many service people will you provide, including servers, bartender, clean-up-crew, and so forth? How will they be dressed? Are they experienced?

- Is your company bonded and do you have liability insurance?

- May we see your current county health permit?

- May we take any left-over food dishes, plus any opened or un-opened bottles of wine or champagne for which we paid?

- When is your deadline for final guest count?

- What is your total price, including all taxes, gratuities, and any extras?

- When are payments due? How much deposit is required?

- What is your refund policy in case of cancelation?

||||||||||||||||||||||||||||||||||||||||||||||||||||||||||||||||||||||||||||||||||||||||||||||||||||||

What the Groom Needs to Know

Get involved when it comes to selecting the food dishes for your reception. Take part in the tastings and don't be cajoled into accepting super-gourmet items, such as miniature crescent rolls filled with caviar in mint sauce.

Also, be the one in charge of the play lists for your reception, whether you hire a band or a DJ. In fact, create a "do not play" list, as well as a "must play" list. While you're at it, have a discussion about the volume of the music.

||||||||||||||||||||||||||||||||||||||||||||||||||||||||||||||||||||||||||||||||||||||||||||||||||||||

Pastry Chef/Bakery

You may purchase your wedding cake, or other pastries, from your reception venue, your caterer, or a local bakery. Again, ask for referrals from friends and other brides. Ask these questions before you hire a pastry chef or bakery:

- What is the total cost for the cake, including delivery and setup at the reception venue?

- Do you require a deposit? When is the balance due?

- May we taste the various types of cake and filling before placing our order?

- What is your policy regarding the return of plastic tier plates, columns, or bridges?

- Will you provide take-home boxes for the top layer and any leftover cake?

- What are your refund and cancellation policies?

Money-Saving Tips

Order or make your own dummy wedding cake (made out of Styrofoam cake layers, and frosted in the normal way). Serve the guests from bakery or homemade sheet cakes, served on elegant paper plates out of the kitchen. Insert a section of real cake into the bottom layer of Styrafoam. Frost over the section so that it isn't visible to your guests. Mark the section in an inconspicuous way so you and your groom know where to cut the cake during the cake-cutting ceremony.

Instead of a pricey cake top, use fresh flowers and ribbon on the top layer. You can also use a wine goblet filled with fresh flowers, standing on a small circular mirror. Another idea is to imbed votive candles on the top of the cake, plus around all the layers. Have someone light all of the candles before the cake cutting ceremony. This gives the illusion of a "flaming cake." Additional ideas for toppers are a Precious Moments figurine, set on a mirror; a blown glass figurine, such as two hearts intertwined or love doves; or a rotating music box, set on a mirror (appoint someone to wind up the music box ahead of time and turn it on during the cake cutting ceremony). As a nod to your family, you may use your mother's or grandmother's cake top.

Instead of pouring champagne for each guest, serve a less expensive champagne punch. Here is my very own "secret" wedding punch recipe:

For every 60 servings

1. Kool-Aid (Make the Kool-Aid ahead of time by mixing the powder with water according to directions on the can.)
2. Add a half gallon sherbet.
3. Add two large bottles of generic lemon-lime soda, plus one bottle champagne.

This punch can be made with raspberry Kool-Aid and raspberry sherbet; lime Kool-Aid and lime sherbet; or lemon Kool-Aid and lemon sherbet. Instead of using regular ice in the punch, which tends to water it down, freeze cubes of the Kool-Aid ahead of time. The beauty of this punch is that once you've added scoops of sherbet and poured ice-cold soda over the top of it, the punch will foam, bubble, and look like a very expensive concoction. You can omit the champagne if you like, or serve from two punch bowls, one with and one without the champagne.

Here's another clever idea: use an ice sculpture as your centerpiece on your buffet table. Sound expensive? It's really not if you make your own. Go to a wedding supply store and purchase a mold. They come in various sizes and shapes, including my favorite: a bride and groom standing together. Simply fill the mold with clear or colored water and freeze solid. Then, when you arrive at your reception venue, remove the mold, according to the directions, and place the sculpture on your buffet table. We used this idea for our daughter's wedding reception and it gave the entire venue an upscale ambience.

A couple more tips: If your champagne will be tray-served, tell the caterer you want the wait staff to fill each champagne glass only two-thirds full. If you're planning a breakfast buffet wedding reception, serve a lighter, less expensive cake, filled and topped with fruits, such as berries, and served with sherbet or whipped cream topping.

Florist

An ultraformal or formal wedding requires the highest standards in floral decorations. These standards apply to the quality of the flowers, the creative artistry of each bouquet and arrangement, and the services of a specialist, known as a professional floral designer. A floral designer works exclusively by contract, usually out of his or her private studio. (Ask your wedding coordinator for referrals.)

A less formal wedding requires less expertise which may be provided by your local florist, or, if you're lucky, talented friends and relatives. They may donate flowers from their gardens, as well as the labor to assemble the bouquets, decorations, and other arrangements. Or, you may purchase your flowers from a wholesale flower market, your local florist, or your supermarket, to be assembled by your talented helpers.

Another option is to order the "really important" flowers, such as the bride's and bridesmaids' bouquets and the men's boutonnieres, from a professional florist and the remaining flowers from a less expensive source, to be arranged by friends and relatives.

When you enter a flower shop for the first time, how does it feel? Are the displays creative and appealing? Do any of the fresh flowers seem droopy? Does the florist seem harried and rushed, or does he or she take plenty of time to answer your questions in a professional manner?

Ask these questions before hiring a florist:

- Can the florist offer referrals from other brides and grooms?
- How experienced is the florist?
- How many weddings has he done and can he provide photos of these wedding flowers?
- Do you offer any wedding packages? If so, what quality of flowers is included? (You can specify that certain flowers are not acceptable.)
- What are the itemized costs?
- What are your refund and cancellation policies?

Be sure to verify all dates, times, and addresses for floral deliveries, plus the names of the delivery person and the person who'll be responsible for placing the arrangements.

‖‖‖

Etiquette 101

Don't order flowers just because they are pleasing to your eye; smell them first. Surprisingly, not all flowers produce a pleasant fragrance, such as the Starburst lily, Rubrim lily, narcissus, and daisies. Daisies should also be avoided for a formal wedding because they denote a "folksiness," which is not what you want at all. Personally, I don't care for the fragrance of carnations, which is another flower considered too "downscale" for an "upscale" wedding.

‖‖‖

Basic floral needs for a typical wedding

Most wedding celebrations include the following floral pieces:

- Bridal bouquet.
- Bridal attendants' bouquets.
- Boutonnieres for all the men, including the groom, his attendants, the fathers, grandfathers, and every man or boy who will be included in your wedding, such as ring bearer, soloist, reader, or candle-lighter.
- Altar arrangements.
- Flower girl basket.
- Corsages for mothers, grandmothers, and every female who will be included in your wedding, such as a soloist, organist, candle-lighter, or reader.
- Floral treatments for candelabras, candle sconces, pews, garlands, unity candle and tapers, and memorial wreaths/candles, if applicable.

‖‖‖

Money-Saving Tips

Do you have a friend or relative with a green thumb who will donate fresh flowers for your wedding? For example, maybe your Aunt Matilda grows roses in her back yard and would love to donate all the yellow roses you need for your big day. If you begin planning your wedding a year in advance, flowers or bulbs can be planted in your own yard in time for your wedding day.

Another source of free flowers is your ceremony venue, which may already have fresh flowers on display that will work with your wedding colors. For example, they may have the front of the church filled with white lilies, and all you'll need to do is wrap them with the ribbon of your choice. Also, find out if your church has another wedding planned for the day of your wedding, because the altar or pew floral arrangements may be able to be used for both weddings, saving both parties money.

If you have someone available who will arrange the flowers the day before the wedding, appoint someone to purchase flowers from the local wholesale flower mart. Many are open to the public. Arm bouquets are popular right now and can be made up the morning of the wedding. An "armful" of fresh flowers may be tied with satin ribbon and used as bouquets for the bride and bridesmaids. At my son's wedding, my daughter-in-law's aunt brought a box of fresh tulips from a florist. She tied several tulips together at the stems with ribbons and handed them to the bride and each bridesmaid.

Make up silk flower arrangements, bouquets, boutonnieres, and centerpieces ahead of time. Order the rest of the wedding flowers from a florist, such as the bridal bouquet, mothers' and grandmothers' corsages, and so on.

Another idea is to substitute less expensive alternatives to the bridal and bridesmaids' bouquets. For example, a white fan decorated with flowers or, for a December wedding, white fur muffs or decorated candy canes. Another popular option is for the bride to carry her Bible or prayer book decorated with streaming ribbons and a single orchid on top.

Additional decorations

You will need to rent or purchase additional decorative items, depending on the style and formality of your wedding, such as:

- Silk or fresh floral garlands that can be draped over windows and doorways, or from pew to pew.

- Balloons.
- Fabric or lace to drape over the altar.
- Candles.
- Strings of tiny white decorator lights.
- White garden trellis or latticework.
- Decorated wedding arch.
- Tissue wedding bells.
- Decorated floral wreaths.
- White or wrought iron benches.
- Old-fashioned street lamps.
- Carousel horses.
- White pillars, urns, or candelabras.
- Wishing well.
- Gazebo.
- Fountains.
- White or gold bird cages.
- White folding chairs.

Money-Saving Tips

Purchase your wedding cake, flowers, and reception food from your favorite supermarket. The bakery department has many cake options, the floral department takes special wedding orders all the time, and the deli is a dependable source for a buffet luncheon reception. Another option is to combine deli offerings with your family's favorite homemade delicacies, or combine supermarket flowers with fresh flowers from your garden.

Make good use of helium balloons. You would be surprised how effective they can be when used in large numbers. For example, helium balloons, when attached to a fishing line held down at each end with covered bricks, will form a natural arch all by themselves. In fact, with no help from you at all, they will *insist* on arching at the center, a convenient law of physics that will enable you to create archways all over the venue: over the head table; the receiving line;

the cake table; and for the wedding party to walk under as they make their grand entrance into the reception venue. Also, consider covering the ceiling with helium-filled balloons, tied with long ribbons dangling down over the heads of the guests. Not only will the ceiling be a mass of color during the reception, but at the end of the reception, each guest is invited to "catch" a balloon to take outdoors and release into the sky as the bride and groom make their getaway.

Musicians

Your choice of musicians will depend on the formality and theme of your ceremony and reception. An informal wedding ceremony may only require a soloist accompanied by guitar, a single pianist, or organist. A more formal ceremony may lend itself to a trained choir, professional singers, and musicians, such as harpist and violinists. An informal reception may only require background music, provided by a DJ or a pianist. A more formal reception may require one or more live bands or orchestral groups, plus specialty performers, such as a bagpiper.

Hiring one or more musicians requires plenty of referrals, not only from the musicians themselves, but from other brides and grooms. It also requires that you actually listen to the musician(s) in person, preferably by discretely listening in on another wedding's ceremony or reception.

If you're planning a religious ceremony at a house of worship, contact your rabbi, priest, or minister for approval of your ceremony musical selections.

Questions you should ask before hiring your musicians include:

- May we audition the group, either during a live performance or by watching a video? (Are they skilled and professional? Do they dress appropriately? Is their music too loud?)
- Will the musician(s) be willing to play your favorite selections? (You may need to purchase sheet music for a few selections.)
- Exactly how many hours will they perform? How long will their breaks be and how many will they take?
- What will they wear?

- What equipment will the musicians bring with them, such as their own sound system? What equipment will we be required to furnish?

- How much room do they need?

- What is their total fee? How much deposit is required? When is the balance due?

- What about gratuities? Are they included in the contract price?

- Do they charge for overtime?

- What are their refund and cancellation policies?

Also, unless you're absolutely, positively, unequivocally sure you can do it without crying or butchering the song, don't plan on singing at your own ceremony. Save it for the reception when you're not as stressed out.

Money-Saving Tips

Within your circle of friends, or with help from your local university's music department, you may be able to locate musicians who will perform for free as recital credit or for a small gratuity. You may also have talented friends or family members who will offer to sing or play a musical instrument at your wedding.

Another money-saver is to hire all or some of the musicians to do double-duty: perform at the ceremony and the reception. For example, if you're already paying the organist for the ceremony, and that person also plays the piano, ask him or her to perform on the piano during the reception.

Photographer

You may have one or more amateur photographers in your family who volunteer to photograph your ceremony. If you decide to go this route, be sure you've seen this person's work. Does it meet your expectations? Is the person experienced and reliable? On the other hand, if you decide to hire a professional photographer, again ask for referrals.

Before hiring a photographer, ask:

- May we see examples of recent weddings you've photographed?
- Are you familiar with the latest trends and special effects in wedding photography?
- What type of cameras do you use? What type of equipment will you be bringing?
- What are the prices of your wedding packages, and exactly how many prints are included in each?
- May we see the quality of the photo albums included in your packages?
- When will you arrive at the ceremony venue, and how many assistants will you provide?
- What will you wear?
- May we furnish a list of personalized photo requests to be added to your standard list?
- How much deposit is required, and when will the balance be due?
- When will the prints be delivered after the wedding? Will you also share them digitally so they may be uploaded to our wedding Website? Do you have a Website where the photos may be viewed and ordered online by family and friends?
- What are your refund and cancellation policies?

Etiquette 101

It's considered poor etiquette to keep your guests waiting at the reception site while you're having photos taken at the ceremony site. One popular solution is to plan as many pre-ceremony photos as possible. To pull this off, you'll need to arrive at the ceremony venue in plenty of time for these important pre-ceremony photos:

- The bride with her attendants.
- The bride with her parents and siblings.
- The groom with his groomsmen and ushers.
- The groom with his parents and siblings.

If the bride and groom don't mind seeing each other before the ceremony, all the formal photographs can be taken beforehand.

Until you do arrive at the reception venue, keep your guests happy with a cocktail hour or hors d'oeuvre and beverage service.

Videographer

You may have one or more amateur videographers in your family who volunteer to record your ceremony and reception. If you've seen their videos or movies and like what they've done, that may be all you need. However, a professional videographer will usually provide a great deal more when it comes to artistry, special effects, and services, such as editing, animated titles, musical enhancements, and—very important—fully charged, dependable battery packs! Another option is to enlist the services of one amateur and one professional. If you decide to hire one professional only, ask for plenty of referrals.

Before hiring a videographer, be sure to ask:

- Do you provide wireless microphones for the bride, groom, and officiant?

- Will you have an adequate number of charged battery packs with you?

- What are the prices of your various packages and what do they include?

- What sites will you cover? (Bride's home? Ceremony and reception venues?)

- Exactly when will you arrive and when will you leave each venue? (Be sure the videographer is committed to stay long enough to shoot your cake cutting, plus your getaway at the end of the reception.)

- What will you wear?

- What amount of deposit is required, and when is final payment due?

- What are your refund and cancellation policies?

Don't hire a photographer or videographer unless you feel comfortable with him or her. Some photographers, for example, have a loud, drill sergeant personality. It's poor etiquette for the members of your wedding party and your wedding guests to be ordered around, so look for someone who is soft-spoken and polite.

Establish a dress code for all vendors and service providers who will be seen by your guests. For example, if you're planning a formal wedding, you don't want your videographer showing up in jeans and tennis shoes.

||||||||||||||||||||||||||||||||||||||||||||||||||||||||||||||||||||||||||||||||||||||||||||||||||||

Money-Saving Tips

Hire a professional photographer or videographer only for your ceremony, and ask trusted friends and relatives to bring their cameras and camcorders to the reception so they can photograph and record your special moments.

Have your photographer place the digital photos on his Website so that any friends or family members who want to order prints may do so at their own expense.

||||||||||||||||||||||||||||||||||||||||||||||||||||||||||||||||||||||||||||||||||||||||||||||||||||

Limousine Rental Company

You may decide to hire one or more limousines, or other form of transportation, such as horse-drawn carriage or a trolley car for transporting:

- Bride and her father to the ceremony venue.
- Mother of the bride and the bride's attendants to the ceremony venue.
- Groom and his attendants to the ceremony venue.
- Bride, groom, and wedding party from ceremony to reception venue.
- A getaway vehicle for the bride and groom following the reception.

Ask other brides and grooms for referrals. Be sure the company is a member of your local Better Business Bureau.

Before hiring a limousine service, ask these questions:

- How long have you been in business?
- Are your drivers professionally attired?
- What is the make and model of your vehicle?
- What is your total cost?
- When is the deposit due? When is final payment due?
- What are your refund and cancellation policies?

What the Groom Needs to Know

You may be legally responsible to see to it that your reception guests don't drive home drunk. Therefore, you may elect to pay your limo driver an extra fee to be available after the reception for any guests who need a ride.

Here are some alternatives to renting the standard limo:

- Borrow a convertible.
- Decorate a pickup truck by skirting and ballooning the bed of the truck where the bride and groom sit on decorated lawn chairs for the wedding parade after the reception.
- How about an old-fashioned hay ride in a hay wagon? This is a great idea for an outdoorsy wedding, especially if it takes place on a farm, ranch, or at any rural venue. Speaking of farms and ranches, how about making your getaway on a tractor?!
- If you're planning a winter wedding and you know there will be snow on the ground, borrow a snowmobile or rent a horse-drawn sleigh.
- Do you know anyone who collects classic or antique cars? One of these beauties is an obvious choice. Call your local classic car club where you may find an owner who is so into his vehicle he is willing to serve as your driver.
- How about galloping off on horseback? Of course, this requires a few minor elements: horses, saddles, and a bride and groom who know how to ride. Braid the horses' tails and manes with white satin ribbons.

- Depending on your hobbies and professions, you may come up with other novelty forms of transportation, such as a decorated bicycle-built-for-two, a yellow school bus, or a fire engine.

Insurance Agent

You probably wonder why you need an insurance agent—well, it's *not* because I expect the stress of the wedding to kill you off! But you do need wedding day insurance. It's relatively affordable and can save all kinds of grief in case the wedding is canceled, someone falls and is injured during the ceremony, your dog bites the officiant, and so on. Look into it! You'll feel really proud that you did such a smart thing!

There are two kinds of wedding insurance:

1. A rider that can be attached to your existing homeowner's or renter's insurance policy that will protect the value of your wedding gifts. This is the least expensive type of wedding insurance.

2. A full-coverage wedding policy that includes lost or stolen gifts, plus any non-refundable expenses in case of a canceled wedding. It also includes liability insurance for mishaps that may take place during the ceremony and reception, and problems you may have with a vendor or service provider. Contact your personal insurance agent, or Fireman's Fund Insurance Company, who underwrites a policy called "weddingsurance."

You also may want to purchase honeymoon travel insurance from an agent, as opposed to purchasing it through the travel agency that books your honeymoon travel.

Vendor Contracts

Get everything in writing, even items you may casually discuss and agree on that aren't usually part of a contract. It's difficult to come back after the fact and say, "But I remember distinctly you said your staff would stay to clean up the kitchen." It's amazing how verbal agreements can be conveniently forgotten.

Don't hire anyone who seems to be in a rush or talks down to you. If you don't have good feelings about the person or the company, keep looking until you feel comfortable with your choice.

Before signing a contract, ask to see the company's current business license. Be sure all contracts are signed and initialed if any changes are made just prior to the signing. If a vendor or service provider refuses to sign a contract, don't do business with him or her. Finally, don't sign anything until you've checked with your local Better Business Bureau and your state's Department of Consumer Affairs. If there's even one complaint filed against the company, consider it a caution.

|||||||||||||||||||||||||||||||||||||||||||||||||||||||||||||||||||||||||||||||||||||||||||||||||||||||||||||||||||

Etiquette 101

It's considered poor etiquette for a wedding vendor or service provider to insinuate him- or herself into the wedding festivities, by socializing or flirting with your guests or any other wedding professionals present or—and this is the worst offense—by offering a toast to the bride and groom.

|||||||||||||||||||||||||||||||||||||||||||||||||||||||||||||||||||||||||||||||||||||||||||||||||||||||||||||||||||

Tipping Guidelines

The following guidelines aren't set in stone, but will give you a general idea of how much you should tip your vendors and service providers:

- Caterer: 5 to 20 percent of his total fee.
- Hairdresser: 10 to 20 percent of total costs.
- Officiant: $25 (in addition to the officiant's standard fee).
- Ceremony musicians: 15 percent of total fees.
- Reception musicians: $30 to $50 per musician.
- Photographer/videographer: $100 each, only if you are hiring them on a flat fee.
- Wedding coordinator: 15 percent of his or her total fees.
- Transportation driver: 20 percent of total fees.
- Waiters/bartenders: $20 to $25 each.

Plan your tipping in advance so that you have cash on hand to use as tips. You may want to prepare envelopes designated ahead of time for each service provider. If one of your service providers does *not* deserve a tip, stash the cash in your wallet to spend on your honeymoon. Tips are meant to reward excellent service.

Chapter 3

Pre-Wedding Parties

It's party time, and you're the guests of honor. You'll be in demand for engagement parties, bridal showers, co-ed parties, bachelor and bachelorette parties, a bridal luncheon, and the wedding rehearsal dinner. Here's what to expect:

Engagement Parties

The purpose of an engagement party, of course, is to celebrate your engagement, but it's also a chance for the two families to meet and get to know each other. It can be a formal or informal get-together, and may be hosted and attended by friends or family. Traditionally, however, it has been a formal party hosted by the bride's or groom's parents and attended by members of the couple's families. This is usually a sit-down dinner, followed by dessert and coffee where chit-chat takes place between family members.

Informal options are also popular, such as a barbecue or Hawaiian luau around the pool, or a get-acquainted party in a home setting where the couple's memorabilia is on display. For example, you might find your Little League uniform, cheerleading pom-poms, awards, trophies, photos, yearbooks, and so forth.

Toasts are in order during any engagement party, usually offered by the fathers of the bride and groom.

Etiquette 101

Rules of etiquette for a formal engagement party:

- The bride and groom must attend all engagement parties together.

- Everyone invited to an engagement party must also be invited to the wedding.

- The party should be tasteful. For example, it would be in poor taste to give the bride a gift of a negligee, or the groom something risqué that would be more appropriate for a bachelor party.

- Appropriate engagement gifts may be precious family heirlooms being handed down by a relative, or sentimental gifts that will be treasured for a lifetime, such as an elegantly framed engagement photo, or a pillow embroidered with the couple's names and wedding date.

- If only a few guests bring gifts, do not open them during the party, because this may embarrass those who didn't bring gifts. Open the gifts after all the guests have left.

- A formal engagement party requires that the invitation be engraved or handwritten by a calligrapher. A less formal party invitation may be computer-generated, handwritten, or extended by phone or e-mail.

Engagement toasts

Here are a couple toasts that would be appropriate at an engagement party:

"No sooner met, but they looked; no sooner looked but they loved; no sooner loved but they sighed; no sooner knew the reason but they sought the remedy." These are the words of Shakespeare, but aren't they true of [couple's names], for "no sooner looked but they loved." May we call it "love at first sight"? I think so. We all raise our glasses in a toast to you, [couple's names], as we celebrate your engagement. Congratulations!

[Couple's names], it is an honor to toast to your engagement. May this be the start of something wonderful, a brand-new life, a beautiful beginning. Here's to a future filled with romance, delight, sharing, laughter, and great adventure, as your love grows with each passing day.

Etiquette 101

Some things to remember for pre-wedding parties:

- Although proper etiquette dictates that the bride and groom should write thank-you notes to each person who hosts a pre-wedding party, and to everyone who brings a gift, that rule has been softened somewhat in today's society. Today the only thank-you note actually required is to the party hosts and to anyone who sent a gift to the party, but was unable to attend. Everyone else can be thanked during the party.

- It's considered poor etiquette for the couple to host their own engagement party.

- At a formal bridal tea, the maid or matron of honor is expected to pour the tea. If she isn't present, the hostess may pour.

- Other than members of the wedding party, the same guests should not be invited to multiple parties.

Bridal Showers

This is the party where the bride is "showered" with affection, support, and thoughtful, loving gifts. The gifts usually match the theme and formality of the party. Here are a couple common themes:

- Formal bridal tea. This is the most elegant bridal shower, not only attended by the bride's friends, but mothers, sisters, aunts, and grandmothers. The gifts usually relate to tea parties: lace tablecloth, family heirloom tea cup and saucer set, a cut crystal vase, and so forth.

- Informal parties. Themes range from kitchen shower, to honeymoon trousseau, to linen shower, to a recipe shower. They may be held in a home, at a restaurant, or at the office during the lunch break.

Co-Ed Parties

This is an informal boy/girl party with plenty of food and fun. Gifts for the couple abound as well, but the emphasis is on the eats and activities. It can be a beach party, a scavenger hunt, miniature golf party, pizza party, or a bon voyage party for the couple who may be cruising on their honeymoon. Gifts are usually clever and practical, such as swim towels and underwater goggles for a travel party, or a his-and-her-tool party, where they receive gifts for the workshop and the kitchen.

Bridal Luncheon

The bridal luncheon, also called the bridesmaids' luncheon, differs from the typical bridal shower in several ways. The guests are a select group, usually composed of the bride and her attendants, although in certain parts of the country and within certain ethnic groups, it's considered proper etiquette to invite the mothers of the bride, groom, flower girl, ring bearer, and the couple's sisters. This luncheon is usually held closer to the wedding day than a bridal shower, especially if the bride's attendants must travel to the wedding.

The luncheon is hosted by the maid or matron of honor, with help from the bridesmaids, or it may be hosted by the bride herself. It usually takes place in an upscale restaurant, tearoom, or in a private home. Gifts are exchanged during this party. The bridesmaids present the bride with a joint gift, usually something special for the bride to wear during the wedding or honeymoon, and the bride presents individual gifts, usually a piece of jewelry to be worn during the wedding, such as matching pearl necklaces.

A tradition during a bridal luncheon is to serve a pink cake with small charms hidden between the layers, each attached to a ribbon. Each charm has a special meaning: a four-leaf clover means good luck, a heart means love is on the horizon, and the wedding ring charm is said to determine the next to wed.

||||||||||||||||||||||||||||||||||||||||||||||||||||||||||||||||||||||||||||||||||||||||||||||||||||||||

Etiquette 101

Party expenses are paid by the person or group hosting the event. In the case of the bridal luncheon, for example, if the bridesmaids are hosting, they pay; if the bride is hosting, she pays.

||||||||||||||||||||||||||||||||||||||||||||||||||||||||||||||||||||||||||||||||||||||||||||||||||||||||

Bachelorette Party

The traditionally rowdy bachelorette party, with male strippers or an X-rated movie, has given way to a day at the spa, lunch, and a shopping spree; an evening at a live musical or theatrical performance; or a day on the ski slopes. It's considered more of a fun escape than an actual party, usually several hours spent together doing something special. It's often scheduled to coincide with the groom's bachelor party.

Bachelor Party

No longer considered a "last night out with the boys," complete with a keg and a stripper who jumps out of a cake, the trend is more toward sports-oriented get-togethers, casino weekends, poker parties, or good, old-fashioned roasts. It's a great time for the guys to get together before the big day, and it includes the groom's close friends, members of his wedding party, his father, and brothers of the bride and groom. It may be hosted by the groom, the best man, or the groom's father.

Instead of planning the bachelor party on the night before the wedding, it makes more sense to have it a day or two or three before, because not only is the night before the wedding usually reserved for the wedding rehearsal and the rehearsal dinner, but it's an awesome idea to avoid a hangover. During the bachelor party, it's traditional for the groom to toast his bride, even though she isn't present. All he needs to do is raise his glass and say, "To my bride," which will be followed by the rest of the guests who will join him in the toast.

The Wedding Rehearsal

The time of the rehearsal should be convenient for everyone, especially the officiant. Hopefully, the rehearsal can be held early enough in the evening to allow for a relaxing dinner afterward.

Whether your wedding will be formal or informal, certain rules of etiquette apply when it comes to such things as conducting the rehearsal, hosting the dinner, and offering toasts. A rehearsal is a joyous time, marking the end of many long months of anticipation and tedious planning. It's a time for everyone in the wedding party to meet and socialize, sometimes for the first time.

The purpose of the rehearsal is to run through the ceremony from start to finish, including the processional, recessional, and the order of service. Each member of the wedding party needs to know when to walk, how to walk, and where to stand during the ceremony. The bride and groom need to feel comfortable with the officiant and the sequence of events. They also need to know when to speak, when to be silent, and when to move, including such things as lighting the unity candle or circling the altar three times, as required by certain religious faiths.

The musicians, as well as anyone who will recite a poem or read from scripture, also need to rehearse. The rehearsal is a must for any children involved in the ceremony, including candle lighters, junior ushers or bridesmaids, the flower girl, ring bearer, and train bearers. The train bearers can practice carrying a length of fabric that has been tied to the bride's waist. (A single bed sheet will work.)

The bride usually carries a pretend bridal bouquet (created from bridal shower ribbons and bows) as she practices walking down the aisle, handing it off to her honor attendant during the ceremony, then retrieving it before the recessional.

The bride and groom don't actually recite their vows during the rehearsal, but listen to the officiant who goes over them briefly. If the bride and groom have written their own vows, they can practice in private before the wedding day.

The rehearsal is an opportune time to deliver checks to anyone who is being paid to participate, such as a soloist, organist, or harpist.

It's a nice touch if your photographer and videographer can be present to capture the candid moments that always take place during a rehearsal. If this isn't possible, ask friends and relatives to bring their cameras and camcorders; you can also provide disposable cameras to anyone present.

Etiquette 101

If the rehearsal is being held in a house of worship, find out ahead of time if there is a dress code for those in attendance. Some churches don't allow super casual attire, such as cutoffs, tank tops, or flip-flops, even during a wedding rehearsal.

The officiant usually conducts the rehearsal, along with the wedding co-ordinator, if you choose to hire one. A coordinator will help the wedding party line up, establish a pace for the processional, and so on.

Everyone involved in the wedding ceremony should attend, including the officiant, attendants, musicians, bride, groom, their parents, and any other participants.

This is the time the groom or the best man should deliver two things to the officiant: a check for his or her services and the original signed marriage license.

The Rehearsal Dinner

The dinner takes place following the wedding rehearsal. It may take place at the ceremony venue, such as the church's fellowship hall, or at a restaurant or a private home.

It may be formal or informal and is usually hosted and paid for by the groom's parents. If a formal dinner, it should not be more formal than the wedding reception. Depending on the circumstances, it may be hosted by the bride's parents, bride's or groom's grandparents, an aunt and uncle, or as a joint venture between both sets of parents. A successful rehearsal dinner offers a comfortable setting where everyone can relax, get to know each other, and enjoy each other's company before the big day.

Although the guest list will be relatively small, invitations are required and it's important that everyone be invited who should be invited, including the bride and groom, their parents, all wedding attendants and their spouses, the clergyman and spouse, the parents of any children who are participating in the ceremony, plus any special out-of-town guests, including grandparents or aunts and uncles.

A rehearsal dinner invitation may read like this:

Joseph and Melanie Peterson
invite you to the rehearsal dinner
in honor of
Ashley and Jason
Friday, September 18th at 6:30 p.m.
The Stakeout Restaurant
9182 East Williamsburg Avenue
Trenton, Virginia

Toasts are usually offered during a rehearsal dinner; the best man toasts the bride and groom, the groom toasts his bride and her parents, the bride toasts her groom and his parents.

Toast to the bride and groom from the best man

"I would like to propose a toast to Ashley and Jason. It's an honor to be asked to serve as best man. Thank you. May your wedding day be perfect in every way. To Ashley and Jason."

Toast from the groom to his bride and her parents

"I would like to propose a toast to Ashley and her wonderful parents, Joe and Melanie. You have been such positive role models in Ashley's life. I'm proud to become your son-in-law. Thanks for all the help you've been to us as we've planned our wedding. I love you very much. To my bride and her awesome parents."

Toast from the bride to her groom and his parents

"I would like to propose a toast to Jason and his parents. Jeffrey and Sandra, thank you for raising such a special man. I love him dearly and I am blessed to become part of your family. Thank you for all the help you've given us as we've planned our wedding. I love you very much. To my groom and his incredible parents."

The rehearsal dinner is an opportunity to make introductions all around, affording the bride's and groom's relatives a chance to get to know each other. Various family members may tell interesting or humorous anecdotes about the bride and groom when they were young, along with childhood photos of the couple. The rehearsal dinner is an opportune time for the bride and groom to thank those present who helped with the wedding preparations. The bride and groom may distribute their thank-you gifts to members of their wedding party, if they haven't done so already. Here are popular choices:

For the bride's attendants

- A piece of jewelry to be worn during the wedding, such as a pearl necklace or earrings.
- Collectible silver spoons.
- Collectible figurines, such as Precious Moments.
- Music box.
- Jewelry box.
- Gift certificate to Bath and Body Works.

For the groom's attendants

- Pewter tankards.
- Briefcase or laptop case.
- For the guy who barbecues: barbecue tools, chef's hat, gourmet sauces, customized apron.
- For the golfer: balls, towel, golf gloves.
- For the fisherman: lures, flies, vest, rod case.
- For the indoor sportsman: chess set, mug with his favorite team's logo, sports trivia book.
- For the coffee lover: gift certificate to Starbucks, gourmet coffee beans, electric coffee grinder.

For the girls (depending on age)

- Collector dolls (such as Madame Alexander).
- Heart-shaped locket.
- Stuffed animal.
- Toys.

- Bath basket (bubble bath, shower gel, decorative soaps, candles, rubber duckies).
- Beach basket (beach towel, tanning lotion, visor, sunglasses, flip-flops, Frisbee).

For the boys (depending on age)

- Collector baseball, football, or basketball cards.
- Other collector sports memorabilia.
- Sports equipment (depending on the boys' interests).
- Video games.
- Stuffed animal.
- Toys.

For the parents

- Elegant sterling silver frame for the wedding invitation or favorite wedding photo.
- Keepsake box, to be filled with memorabilia from the wedding, such as Dad's pressed boutonniere, Mom's preserved corsage, invitation, ceremony program, snips of ribbon and other items from the ceremony and reception decor, such as wedding favors or small white wedding bells.
- Wedding memory topiary. This is a silk or live indoor tree decorated with similar items.
- Live wedding tree. This is an evergreen tree to be planted in a decorative pot or in the parent's garden in remembrance of your wedding day. It will always be green, a symbol of the couple's everlasting love and appreciation for their parents, plus the tree will grow each year, as a symbol of the couple's ever-growing love for each other. Attach a card that expresses these sentiments.

If gift-buying just isn't your thing, you're always safe with tickets to a sports event or the theater, or a gift certificate to a restaurant or an appropriate store.

Pre-Wedding Snacks

Someone needs to furnish pre-wedding finger foods for members of the wedding party to eat after they arrive at the ceremony venue. If it's a morning wedding, provide a simple continental breakfast with coffee, juice, donuts, and breakfast rolls. If the wedding is later in the day, serve small finger sandwiches, plus cookies and fruit. The key is to avoid anything sticky or drippy. Although a small thing, this thoughtful idea is much appreciated before the wedding, and it may keep someone from passing out for lack of food.

Part 2

The Wedding Ceremony

The wedding ceremony is the heart of your wedding day, and you are the stars of the show. As you plan your ceremony, you'll soon discover that it's a major production, where rules of etiquette abound. If you're not especially fond of rules and restrictions, you might want to avoid a religious or ultraformal wedding.

A less formal ceremony, or a civil ceremony that takes place at a secular venue, is much less restrictive. In fact, as the formality decreases, the rules slacken to the point of being practically nonexistent for a casual wedding, such as a surprise wedding or a wedding at the beach.

Here are guidelines for five basic degrees of wedding formality:

1. Ultraformal

    *   A minimum of 200 guests.
    *   Held at an upscale venue, such as a cathedral, synagogue, resort, or country club.
    *   Ten or more total attendants.
    *   Elegant sit-down dinner and ballroom dancing to live music.

2. Formal
    - A minimum of 100 guests.
    - Held at an upscale site, similar to an ultraformal wedding.
    - Six or more total attendants.
    - Sit-down or buffet dinner.
    - Live music or DJ.

3. Semiformal
    - Fewer than 100 guests.
    - Held in a church, outdoors, or other less formal venue.
    - Two or more attendants.
    - Light lunch or finger food reception.
    - Live music or DJ.

4. Informal
    - Fewer than 50 guests.
    - Held in a chapel, a home, or other informal setting.
    - Two attendants total: maid or matron of honor and best man.
    - Light breakfast, brunch, finger food, or dessert-only reception.

5. Casual

    A casual wedding may take place at the top of a ski slope, during a beach party, in a barn, or in your home or backyard—or perhaps around the pool or during a family get-together.

If this isn't your first marriage, Chapter 6 will help you plan an especially meaningful ceremony, including any children from a previous marriage.

Finally, whatever type of ceremony you plan, Chapter 7 provides dozens of ways to personalize your wedding by adding a few of these poignant touches:

- Including your pet in your ceremony.
- Dad's giving-away words.
- Ethnic and cultural traditions.
- Jumping the broom.

- Handfasting ceremony.
- Ceremony of salted bread and grain.
- Ceremony of the silk cord.
- Ceremony of the care cloth.
- Ceremony of the loving cup.
- Ceremony of the blessing stones.
- Ceremony of the unity candle.
- Blessing of the coins.
- Ceremony of salt or sand.
- Life renewal wedding ceremony.

As you plan your ceremony, take plenty of time to consider all your options. I'm sure your ceremony will be distinctive and unique.

Chapter 4

Religious Ceremonies

Most religious venues will provide you with a list of their wedding policies, plus what is or is not allowed to take place on their premises. The first step is to take a look at these requirements before you commit to a religious ceremony. You may decide against a religious ceremony when you find out you'll be obligated to raise your children in this particular faith, or you may object to the religious marriage certificate you'll be required to sign. Or, you may not have realized that pre-marital counseling is required before you can marry.

Once you've made your decision and committed to a religious ceremony, this chapter provides you with the basic etiquette and procedures expected in several different denominations.

Protestant

A Protestant wedding may be more or less restrictive depending on the particular denomination. For example, the Methodist church is less restrictive than the Eastern Orthodox. The first thing you'll find is that a Protestant wedding is almost never allowed on a Sunday. Depending on your clergyman's policy, the wedding may take place in a church or at a secular site.

Most Protestant clergymen require pre-marital counseling before marrying a couple. If you were married before, this is usually not a problem with most Protestant officiants; however, I've heard of ministers who refuse to marry a couple if one or both have been divorced.

There are hundreds of Protestant churches in America, many of which are not affiliated with any particular denomination. Their styles of worship vary, as do their names, such as "Valley Community Church" or "Stoneridge Bible Church." You'll find a typical nondenominational Protestant wedding and ring vow in the Order of Service later in this chapter.

The following are a few examples of the most popular Protestant denominations in America.

Baptist

There are many branches of Baptists, the two largest being the Southern Baptist Convention and the National Baptist Convention. A Baptist wedding ceremony is considered to be a three-way covenant, between the bride, the groom, and God. The ceremony follows the typical Protestant order listed later in this chapter. The ceremony usually takes place at a Baptist church or in a home. The officiant is addressed as "Pastor."

This is an appropriate wedding vow for a Baptist wedding:

I, [groom's name], take thee, [bride's name], to be my wedded wife, to have and to hold, from this day forward, for better, for worse, for richer, for poorer, in sickness, in health, to love and to cherish, till death us do part, according to God's holy ordinance; and thereto I pledge thee my faith.

Episcopalian

The Episcopalian Church in the United States is also known as the Protestant Episcopal Church, a body originally associated with the Church of England. The Episcopalian denomination tends to favor traditional worship services and wedding ceremonies. An appropriate wedding vow is the same as that for a Baptist wedding.

American Lutheran

The Lutheran Church was founded by Martin Luther during the Reformation of the 16th century. There are many types of Lutheran churches in America, some favoring traditional worship services, whereas others prefer a more contemporary style. However, all the various synods adhere to the religious teachings of Martin Luther.

This is one traditionally accepted wedding vow:

I take you, [groom's name], to be my husband from this day forward, to join with you and share all that is to come, and I promise to be faithful to you until death parts us.

Presbyterian

Although there are many types of Presbyterian churches, they all generally adhere to the religious doctrines of John Calvin, a 16th-century French theologian and religious reformer. As is true in the Lutheran church, Presbyterian churches vary greatly in their style of worship.

In the case of a formal Presbyterian wedding ceremony, this is an acceptable wedding vow:

> *I, [bride's name], take you to be my wedded husband, and I do promise and covenant, before God and these witnesses, to be your loving and faithful wife/husband, in plenty and in want, in joy and in sorrow, in sickness and in health, as long as we both shall live.*

Male wedding guests are expected to wear jackets and ties; female guests may wear a dress or skirt and blouse. Also, a Presbyterian officiant should be addressed as "Reverend"; in Canada he or she should be addressed as "Mr." or "Ms." followed by the officiant's last name.

Methodist

The Methodist Church in America is a Protestant Christian denomination with theologies developed from the teachings of John and Charles Wesley. Their worship services, as well as their marriage ceremonies, vary greatly as to their degree of formality.

Here is an acceptable Methodist wedding vow:

> *In the Name of God, I, [groom's name], take you, [bride's name], to be my wife, to have and to hold from this day forward, for better, for worse, for richer, for poorer, in sickness and in health, to love and to cherish, until we are parted by death. This is my solemn vow.*

Male wedding guests are expected to wear a jacket and tie; the women are expected to wear a dress. Also, a Methodist officiant should be addressed as "Reverend" or "Pastor."

United Church of Christ

The United Church of Christ is a fairly new denomination in America, founded in 1957 by a merger between the Congregational Christian Church and the Evangelical and Reformed Church. In the present Book of Worship, published in 1986, their denomination's preferred wedding vows are stated, reflecting the important concept of giving one's self, as different from taking another.

This is a United Church of Christ wedding vow:

[Bride's name], I give myself to you to be your husband. I promise to love and sustain you in the covenant of marriage, from this day forward, in sickness and in health, in plenty and in want, in joy and in sorrow, as long as we both shall live.

Unitarian

The Unitarian Church does not offer a standard service, but leaves the composition of the service to each of its ministers.

Here is a typical Unitarian-Universalist wedding vow:

Minister asks the bride and groom: *Will you take [groom or bride's name] to be your husband/wife; love, honor and cherish him/her now and forevermore?*

Bride and groom answer: *I will.*

Minister asks the bride and groom to repeat these words: *I, [bride or groom's name], take you, [groom or bride's name], to be my husband/ wife; to have and to hold from this day forward, for better or for worse, for richer or for poorer, in sickness and in health, to love and cherish always.*

Quaker

The Quaker faith requires a notice of intent to wed be read at least one month before the wedding in front of a meeting of Society of Friends. The ceremony is quite simple and much less ostentatious than other denominations. The marriage usually takes place during a regular worship meeting where all in attendance meditate silently while the bride and groom enter and join those already seated. Then, after the traditional Quaker silence, the bride and groom rise, join hands, face each other and repeat these vows:

In the presence of God and these our Friends, I take thee to be my wife/husband, promising with Divine assistance to be unto thee a loving and faithful wife/ husband so long as we both shall live.

The groom speaks his promises first; the bride follows. The bride is not given away, nor does a third person pronounce them married, for the Friends believe that only God can create such a union.

A marriage certificate is brought to the couple for them to sign. This certificate includes the vows they have each spoken. When the worship meeting has ended, all present are asked to sign this certificate.

Male guests usually wear jacket and tie; the women wear dresses, skirts and blouses, or pants suits.

||||||||||||||||||||||||||||||||||||||||||||||||||||||||||||||||||||||||||||||||||||||||||||||||||||

Etiquette 101

Many Protestant denominations have dress restrictions for wedding guests. Men are expected to wear a suit and tie or a jacket and tie. The women should have their upper arms covered and their hems should reach below their knees. Shorts are almost never acceptable, even if they are knee-length. In a minority of Protestant denominations, such as the Church of the Brethren, women are expected to wear a head covering.

||||||||||||||||||||||||||||||||||||||||||||||||||||||||||||||||||||||||||||||||||||||||||||||||||||

Protestant wedding services and traditions

Seating

The bride's family is usually seated on the left side of the church or venue (as you face the altar), and the groom's on the right. The parents are usually seated in the front rows, with brothers, sisters, and their spouses in the second rows on each side. The third rows are reserved for grandparents and other close relatives. The remaining rows are for the couple's friends.

||||||||||||||||||||||||||||||||||||||||||||||||||||||||||||||||||||||||||||||||||||||||||||||||||||

Etiquette 101

When the bride's or groom's parents are divorced, the mother is usually seated in the front pew (alone or with her new husband), and the father is seated in the third pew (alone or with his new wife). The rule of thumb is to keep one pew between divorced parents.

If the bride's father is deceased or, if she prefers to have someone else walk her down the aisle, she has several choices: her stepfather, an uncle, a brother, her mother, her groom, or she may walk down the aisle alone.

In the case of an encore wedding, the bride may want her children to walk her down the aisle. If the bride is close to her natural father and her stepfather, she may choose one of them to walk her down the aisle, but she should make a point to include her other dad in some way during the ceremony.

Processional

The processional takes place in this order:

- The clergyman (optional).
- Groomsmen, walking in pairs (optional).
- Junior ushers.
- Junior bridesmaids.
- Bridesmaids, walking in single file or in pairs.
- Honor attendant (maid or matron of honor).
- Ring bearer.
- Flower girl (the ring bearer and flower girl may walk down the aisle side by side). Note: If the flower girl is tossing rose petals, ask her to toss them on the sides of the aisle, not down the center. This will prevent the bride and bridesmaids from slipping on them.
- The bride enters on her father's left arm, followed by train bearers who carry the bridal gown's train.

Typical order of service for a Protestant wedding

The service usual proceeds as follows:

- Prelude and seating of guests.
- Candle lighting.
- Lighting of memorial candle, if applicable.

- Seating of mother of the bride.

- Processional.

- Giving of the bride.

- Prayer.

- Scripture reading.

- Pastoral comments.

- Exchanging of vows and rings.

- Lighting of unity candle, if applicable.

- Pronouncement of marriage.

- Introduction of the bride and groom.

- Recessional.

||||||||||||||||||||||||||||||||||||||||||||||||||||||||||||||||||||||||||||||||||||||||||||||||||||||

What the Groom Needs to Know

Don't worry if the ring doesn't slip easily onto your bride's finger during the ring vows. Without missing a beat, simply place it on her pinkie finger instead, and worry about it later. Talk to your fiancée about it ahead of time so that neither of you is surprised when this common problem arises. Also, ask her to use the same trick if she can't place your ring on your finger easily.

Your marriage license must be signed by two people who witness your marriage ceremony. These witnesses may or may not be your best man and the bride's honor attendant. Once you and your witnesses have signed the license following the ceremony, it's the responsibility of your officiant to mail it in for recording. Once the marriage license has been recorded, an official copy won't necessarily be mailed to you. You may need to request an official copy in order to legally change your bride's name on her driver's license, her social security card, your bank accounts, and on other documents.

||||||||||||||||||||||||||||||||||||||||||||||||||||||||||||||||||||||||||||||||||||||||||||||||||||||

Ceremony convocation/invocation

In a religious ceremony, the convocation and invocation immediately follow the processional. Once the members of the wedding party are in place, the clergyman or officiant speaks, formally convening the marriage service, and invoking God's blessing upon it.

Here are examples of convocations and invocations:

Convocations

We are gathered here today in the presence of these witnesses to join [bride's name] and [groom's name] in holy matrimony, which is commended to be honorable among all men and to be entered into reverently and discreetly.

Friends, we are here to share a very important day in the lives of [bride's name] and [groom's name]—their wedding day. We are honored to be part of this day, to witness their vows and send them off as husband and wife, with our blessings.

We are here today to witness the joining together of [bride's name] and [groom's name] in the holy state of matrimony. We are also here to celebrate with them, and to share their joy.

Invocations

May the God who knows us and loves us grant blessings on [bride's name] and [groom's name] as they become husband and wife this day. And grant your blessings also to this couple's family members and friends, assembled here today for this beautiful ceremony.

God, our Father in heaven, the source of all love, please be present today during this sacred ceremony. We especially ask your blessing on this couple, who stands before us, and for all of us who share their joy. May each one of us sense your love and may we be filled with your love as we witness the vows of [bride's name] and [groom's name]. Amen.

Ceremony consecration and expression of intent

The consecration and expression of intent immediately follow the convocation and invocation. Each officiant has a selection of wordings for the consecration and expression of intent, and he or she will probably allow you to choose which wordings you want included in your ceremony.

A consecration, as it pertains to a marriage ceremony, is the declaration that the ceremony be considered sanctified and dedicated to a sacred purpose: "Our holy God, please sanctify the marriage vows to be spoken today by [bride's name] and [groom's name]. As their vows are spoken, may they not only dedicate themselves to each other, but to You for the sacred purpose of serving You as a married couple.

An expression of intent is exactly what it sounds like: the bride's and groom's verbal expression of intent to marry each other:

Clergyman to the bride: *[Bride's name], is it your intent to marry [groom's name] today? To bond to him as his wife?*

Bride: *Yes.*

Clergyman to the groom: *[Groom's name], is it your intent to marry [bride's name] today? To bond to her as her husband?*

Groom: *Yes.*

Pronouncement of marriage

A wedding officiant, whether religious or secular, uses certain wording for the pronouncement of marriage. Here is an example:

May you keep this covenant you have made. May you bless each other in your marriage, comforting each other when one needs comfort, sharing each other's joys when one needs someone to share them, and helping each other in all your endeavors throughout your married lives together. And now, by the power vested in me by the laws of the state of [state's name], I pronounce you husband and wife. You may kiss your bride.

Benediction

The benediction is given by the officiant after the pronouncement of marriage and the kiss. Here are examples of benedictions:

Whom God hath joined together, let no one put asunder. May the Lord bless you and keep you. May the Lord make His face shine upon you and be gracious unto you. May the Lord lift up His countenance unto you and give you peace.

Dear God, bless [bride's name] and [groom's name] as they leave this place, and bless the family and friends who have come here to share in this great day. May the Lord go with you all.

Bless this marriage we pray. May it be filled with happiness and love. Please walk beside [couple's names] for all of their days together, and may their home be a place of peace and harmony. Amen.

Recessional for a Protestant wedding

The recessional takes place in this order:

- The bride and groom.
- The ring bearer and flower girl.
- The bride's honor attendant.
- The best man.
- The bridesmaids and groomsmen, walking in pairs, the bridesmaids on the groomsmen's right arms.

Etiquette 101

Providing a guest book at the ceremony venue is optional, but if you do provide one for your guests to sign as they arrive for the ceremony, the guest book attendant may stand beside the guest book up until the bride's mother is seated. Then the attendant should be seated, with the hope that any late visitors will see the book and know to sign it before seating themselves in a back row.

After the ceremony, transport the guest book to the reception venue so that any guests who didn't sign before the ceremony may do so there. If no guest book is provided at the ceremony site, one should be provided at the reception site.

Orthodox

Each Orthodox ceremony, whether Greek, Russian, or other, has its own unique traditions concerning the importance of the Holy Trinity, where the couple stands during the ceremony, how the wedding rings are exchanged, the wearing of the crowns, and other strict rituals that must be included.

The marriage ceremony itself is a long ceremony, rich in symbolism. An Orthodox wedding begins with a betrothal ritual that includes the Blessing and Exchange of Rings. The rings are exchanged between bride and groom three times to signify the Holy Trinity.

At the close of this betrothal ritual, there is the Marriage Rite, including the Candles and the Joining of Hands, followed by the Crowning, the Cup and, finally, the Triumphal Procession of Isaiah. The vows themselves are spoken silently during this service, but the couple is considered married when the crowns are finally removed by the priest and he blesses them by saying, "Be though magnified, O bridegroom."

Male wedding guests are expected to wear a jacket and tie. Women should wear a dress or skirt and blouse. Their clothing should cover their arms and their hems should reach below the knee. Also, an Orthodox officiant should be addressed as "Father."

Roman Catholic

The Catholic Church considers marriage as one of the seven sacraments and of great gravity. If you decide to be married in a Roman Catholic church, you'll have a preliminary meeting with the priest to find out what is expected. This meeting should happen at least nine months before the wedding date. Posting of banns will be required each Sunday for three weeks before the wedding. This posting is a notice of intention to marry. Another requirement will probably be premarital counseling, including a discussion of your religious beliefs. These sessions are called the Pre-Cana sessions, which is a series of seminars led by the priest. They are a combination of religious instruction and pre-marital counseling.

If you were married once before in a Catholic ceremony, you'll be required to receive an annulment from the Church, which may be a complicated, time-consuming procedure, so allow plenty of time to get this taken care of before your wedding date. You may also be required to furnish the priest with a copy of your certificate of baptism and confirmation diploma.

A Roman Catholic ceremony usually takes place in a Catholic church or cathedral on a Saturday at noon, and often includes a nuptial mass. Or, it may take place on a Friday evening or early Sunday morning. However, the Friday and Sunday ceremony may not include a mass.

Wedding guests are encouraged to dress modestly and to avoid wearing black. The men may wear jacket and tie; the women may wear a dress, skirt and blouse, or a pants suit. No head coverings are required. Proper etiquette dictates that a priest be addressed as "Father," a bishop be addressed as "Your Excellency," and a cardinal as "Your Eminence."

The processional, recessional, and the seating are similar to those for a Protestant ceremony.

Typical order of service for a Roman Catholic wedding with a mass

The service usual proceeds as follows:

- Prelude.
- Seating of guests.
- Seating of the mother of the bride.
- Introductory rite.
- Processional.
- The priest welcomes the guests.
- Gathering song (optional if processional hymn was sung).
- Penitential rite.
- Opening prayer.
- Liturgy of the Word.
- First reading (from Old Testament).
- Responsorial Psalm (may be sung by a cantor or recited).
- Second reading (from New Testament).
- Gospel acclamation.
- Gospel reading.
- The priest gives a marriage homily.
- The priest asks the bride and groom questions regarding their faithfulness to each other, freedom of choice, and acceptance of and upbringing of children.
- Exchange of consent (the wedding vows).
- General intercessions.
- Liturgy of the Eucharist (Communion).
- Presentation of the gifts and preparation of the altar.
- Eucharist prayer.

- Sanctus.

- Memorial acclamation.

- Great amen

- Communion hymn.

- Concluding rite.

- Final blessing.

- Dismissal.

- Introduction of married couple and the kiss.

- Recessional.

Vows

Two generally acceptable vow phrasings included in a nuptial mass are:

I, [bride's name], take you, [groom's name], for my lawful husband, to have and to hold, from this day forward, for better, for worse, for richer, for poorer, in sickness and health, until death do us part.

I, [groom's name], take you, [bride's name], to be my wife. I promise to be true to you in good times and in bad, in sickness and in health. I will love and honor you all the days of my life.

The priest blesses the wedding rings and then the bride and groom exchange the rings:

Priest: *Now that you have sealed a truly Christian marriage, give these wedding rings to each other, saying after me.*

Groom (addressing his bride): *In the name of the Father, and of the Son, and of the Holy Spirit. Take and wear this ring as a pledge of my fidelity.* The groom places the bride's ring on her finger.

Bride (addressing her groom): *In the name of the Father, and of the Son, and of the Holy Spirit. Take and wear this ring as a pledge of my fidelity.* The bride places the groom's ring on his finger.

Presentation of flowers to Mary, Mother of God

Following the communion rite, the bride alone, or the bride and groom together, lay flowers at the feet of the statue of Mary. The flowers may be the bride's bouquet or a bouquet of flowers that has been specially designed for this purpose. Often, *Ave Maria* is sung during this presentation. The bride and groom may kneel briefly in private prayer once they reach the statue.

Typical order of service for a Roman Catholic wedding without a mass

The service usually proceeds as follows:

- Entrance rite.
- Processional.
- Liturgy of the Word.
- Homily.
- Rite of Marriage.
- General intercessions.
- Lord's Prayer.
- Final blessings.

Depending on the traditions of their particular parish, the bridal couple should meet with their priest, who may allow them to make certain changes or additions to their ceremony, including:

- The order of the processional and/or recessional.
- Personalized wedding vows.
- Choice of scriptural readings.
- Choice of music.
- Choice of prayers.
- Incorporating a Unity Candle ceremony into the service.
- Adding a memorial candle.

A Papal Blessing, a special blessing directly from the Pope, may be obtained for your ceremony. Contact the Chancery Office of your diocese who will provide you with the application, which should be submitted as soon as you've set the date for your wedding. The blessing is recorded on parchment paper that includes the Pope's official raised seal, signature, and blessing.

Jewish

The three main branches of Judaism (Orthodox, Conservative, and Reform), differ in their requirements. The Orthodox branch follows the laws of the Jewish faith most strictly. The Conservative branch follows the laws less strictly than the Orthodox, and the Reform branch is the most liberal. No single set of rules applies to all Jewish weddings. In fact, most individual rabbis and synagogues develop their own interpretations.

A Jewish wedding ceremony is known as *Kiddushin*, which means betrothal and sanctification. It is a holy act, or mitzvah, governed by Jewish law.

Most branches do not allow weddings to take place on the Sabbath or during any holy days, and also require that a Jewish divorce be obtained before a divorced bride or groom may be married. Speak with your rabbi about other stipulations. For example, not all rabbis will perform an interfaith ceremony and usually only the Reform branch will conduct the ceremony in English.

A Jewish wedding may take place in a temple or synagogue, or at a secular site, such as a resort or at your reception location, depending on the accepted dictates of each rabbi.

In the Orthodox and Conservative wedding services, an ancient Aramaic vow is usually recited before the groom places the ring on his bride's finger. This ring vow also serves as the groom's wedding vow. In the Sephardic transliteration, it reads, "*Harey at mekuddeshet li B'taba'at zo ki'dat Moshe V'israel*," which means, "Behold thou art consecrated unto me with this ring according to the law of Moses and of Israel."

In a double-ring ceremony, the bride presents a ring to her groom in the same way, reciting a slightly different vow.

During a Conservative ceremony, these vows are often used, as taken from the Rabbinical Assembly Manual and published by the Rabbinical Assembly in America:

Rabbi (addressing the groom): *Do you, [groom's name], take [bride's name], to be your lawful wedded wife, to love, to honor and to cherish?*

Groom: *I do.*

Rabbi (addressing the bride): *Do you, [bride's name], take [groom's name], to be your lawful wedded husband to love, to honor and to cherish?*

Bride: *I do.*

Rabbi (addressing the groom): *Then, [groom's name], put this ring upon the finger of your bride and say to her: "Be thou consecrated to me, as my wife, by this ring, according to the Law of Moses and of Israel."*

The Rabbi then asks the bride to repeat the following: *May this ring I receive from thee be a token of my having become thy wife according to the Law of Moses and of Israel.*

If two rings are used, the bride may say:

This ring is a symbol that thou art my husband in accordance with the Law of Moses and Israel.

In a Reformed service, there is a distinctly separate wedding vow that is read by the rabbi and affirmed by both the bride and the groom:

O God, supremely blessed, supreme in might and glory, guide and bless this groom and bride. Standing here in the presence of God, the Guardian of the home, ready to enter into the bond of wedlock, answer in the fear of God, and in the hearing of those assembled: Do you, [bride's name], of your own free will and consent, take this man to be your husband, and do you promise to love, honor and to cherish him throughout life?

Jewish wedding ceremony and traditions

If you plan to be married in a Reform or Conservative Jewish ceremony, the bride's family usually sits on the right side of the temple, the groom's on the left (opposite of a Protestant ceremony). However, for an Orthodox ceremony, men sit on one side of the temple and women on the other.

Because the bride's mother and father escort her down the aisle, her mother isn't seated prior to the processional. The same is true of the groom's mother, if the groom chooses to be escorted down the aisle by both parents.

A Reform Jewish processional is usually the same as a Protestant processional. An Orthodox or Conservative processional follows in this order:

- The rabbi.
- The cantor.
- The bride's grandparents, walking side by side with her grandmother on her grandfather's right (optional).
- The groom's grandparents, also walking side by side, his grandmother on his grandfather's right (optional).

- The ushers (groomsmen) walking in pairs.
- The best man, walking alone.
- The groom, escorted down the aisle between his parents (father on his left arm, mother on his right).
- The bridesmaids, walking in pairs.
- The honor attendant walking alone.
- The ring bearer.
- The flower girl.
- The bride escorted down the aisle between her parents (father on her left arm, and her mother on her right).

A typical order of service for a Jewish wedding is as follows:

- Seating of guests.
- Processional.
- The rabbi, the bride, groom, their attendants, and parents stand under the chuppah.
- The bride and groom sip ceremonial wine.
- The bride and groom are blessed by the rabbi.
- The groom gives the bride a gold wedding ring. Rabbi (addressing the groom): "Then, do you, *[groom's name]*, put this ring upon the finger of your bride and say to her: Be thou consecrated to me, as my wife, by this ring, according to the Law of Moses and of Israel."

   The rabbi then asks the bride to repeat the following: "May this ring I receive from thee be a token of my having become thy wife according to the Law of Moses and of Israel."

   If two rings are used, the bride may say: "This ring is a symbol that thou art my husband in accordance with the Law of Moses and Israel."

- The marriage contract (*ketubah*) is read aloud and given to the couple.
- The Seven Blessings are read, during which time the bride and groom sip ceremonial wine from the *kiddush* cups. They may be read by one family member or seven family members, one blessing each: *You Abound in Blessings, Adonai our God, who created the*

fruit of the vine. You Abound in Blessings, Adonai our God. You created all things for Your glory. You Abound in Blessings, Adonai our God. You created humanity. You Abound in Blessings, Adonai our God. You made humankind in Your image, after Your likeness, and You prepared from us a perpetual relationship. You abound in Blessing, Adonai our God. You created humanity. May she who was barren rejoice when her children are united in her midst of joy. You Abound in Blessings, Adonai our God, who makes Zion rejoice with her children. You make these beloved companions greatly rejoice even as You rejoiced in Your creation in the Garden of Eden as of old. You Abound in Blessings, Adonai our God, who makes the bridegroom and bride to rejoice. You Abound in Blessings, Adonai our God, who created joy and sadness, bridegroom and bride, mirth and exultation, pleasure and delight, love, fellowship, peace, and friendship. Soon may there be heard in the cities of Judah and in the streets of Jerusalem, the voice of joy and gladness, the voice of the bridegroom and the voice of the bride, the jubilant voice of bridegrooms from their canopies and of youths from their feasts of song. You Abound in Blessings, Adonai our God. You make the bridegroom rejoice with the bride.

- The groom breaks a glass with his foot (the bride may also participate in this ritual).
- Benediction by the rabbi.
- Recessional.

Meanings of the breaking of the glass

The breaking of the glass is a tradition that has several meanings: It teaches us that life brings us both joy and sadness, such as the destruction of the Second Temple in Jerusalem in AD 70. The sound of the breaking glass is said to frighten away evil spirits so they won't spoil the joy of the wedding day. It demonstrates that love, like glass, is fragile and must be handled with care. It confirms the irrevocable promises made by the bride and groom. Just as the glass is irrevocably broken, so the couple's commitment to each other is also irrevocable.

Recessional for a Jewish wedding

A Jewish recessional takes place in this order:

- The bride and groom.
- The bride's parents.

- The groom's parents.
- The flower girl.
- The ring bearer.
- The bride's honor attendant.
- The best man.
- The bridesmaids, each escorted by an usher (groomsman).
- The last down the aisle are the cantor and the rabbi.

|||||||||||||||||||||||||||||||||||||||||||||||||||||||||||||||||||||||||||||||||||||||||||||||||||||||||||||

Etiquette 101

Male guests must wear a yarmulke for an Orthodox or Conservative wedding ceremony and for some Reform ceremonies. Women are encouraged to wear a dress or skirt and blouse. It should be modest and cover her arms. The hem should reach below her knees. Do not wear jewelry symbolic of any other religion, such as a cross.

|||||||||||||||||||||||||||||||||||||||||||||||||||||||||||||||||||||||||||||||||||||||||||||||||||||||||||||

Elements common to Jewish weddings

Jewish weddings often have meaningful rituals attached to them. Many of these elements date back centuries.

Mikveh (ritual bath)

A day or so before the wedding, the bride is cleansed in a ritual bath, called the Mikveh. This allows her to enter marriage in a pure state. Before her ritual bath, she must remove all rings, hair accessories, bandages, and nail polish, to assure there is no barrier between her body and the cleansing bath.

Ufruf

This is a ritual practiced by Orthodox and Conservative Jews where the groom reads from the Torah and recites the proper blessings over it. The rabbi then has the bride join the groom and he blesses them both for their forthcoming marriage.

Ceremonial wine

The ceremonial wine must be kosher. It may be poured into a decanter prior to the service, which provides formal service, as opposed to serving from the wine bottle. The wine is poured into kiddush cups for the two wine blessings. The first blessing is symbolic of the commitment of the betrothal; the second blessing is symbolic of the commitment of marriage.

Yichud

It is a Jewish tradition for the bride and groom to have a special, quiet time together immediately following the ceremony. Ask your caterer to leave two plates of food for you beforehand so that you may eat your first meal together in private, breaking your fast, if applicable. This *yichud* should take place in a room that can be locked for total privacy.

The chuppah

Unless you're planning a Reform wedding, you'll be required to provide a wedding canopy, also known as a Jewish *chuppah*. (A chuppah is optional for a Reform ceremony.) It may be a piece of fabric or a prayer shawl, supported by a pole on each of four corners. If the rabbi approves, the poles may be decorated with flowers.

The chuppah is a symbolic tradition representing the new home (or tent) of the bride and groom. Often, the parents stand with the couple under the chuppah during the ceremony. While standing under the chuppah, the Seven Blessings are recited.

Yarmulke

The *yarmulke*, also known as a *kipa*, is a skull cap worn by many Jews while praying. It reminds one that God is always above us.

Muslim

A traditional Muslim wedding requires a formal betrothal to take place, followed by the signing of the marriage contract, and then the wedding ceremony itself.

Most Muslim weddings take place inside a mosque, but they may also take place at secular sites. The officiant is usually an *imam*, who is an Islamic religious leader. A Muslim ceremony usually includes a reading from the

Qur'an, plus several prayers. A white cloth may be placed over the heads of the bride and groom while the Qur'an is held above the cloth; this is a symbol of Allah's protection and purity.

Male wedding guests may wear casual shirt and slacks—no head covering required. Female wedding guests should wear a dress or skirt and blouse. Their clothing should cover their arms and hems should reach below the knee. A scarf must cover their heads. Guests are discouraged from wearing visible jewelry, including crosses, Star of David, signs of the zodiac, or pendants with faces or heads of people or animals. The imam who conducts the ceremony may be addressed as "Imam" or by his name.

These are the vows that are spoken:

Bride: *I, [bride's name], offer you myself in marriage in accordance with the instructions of the Holy Qur'an and the Holy Prophet, peace and blessing be upon Him. I pledge, in honesty and with sincerity, to be for you an obedient and faithful wife.*

Groom: *I pledge, in honesty and sincerity, to be for you a faithful and helpful husband.*

Hindu

A Hindu wedding ceremony may take place at any covered venue. The ceremony is quite lengthy, up to three hours long, followed by rituals and activities that may last up to a week.

Here is a modern-day interpretation of the traditionally strict Hindu wedding vows:

Let us take the first steps to provide for our household a nourishing and pure diet, avoiding those foods injurious to healthy living. Let us take the second step to develop physical, mental, and spiritual powers. Let us take the third step, to increase our wealth by righteous means and proper use. Let us take the fourth step, to acquire knowledge, happiness, and harmony by mutual love and trust. Let us take the fifth step, so that we be blessed with strong, virtuous, and heroic children. Let us take the sixth step, for self-restraint and longevity. Finally, let us take the seventh step, and be true companions and remain lifelong partners by this wedlock.

The Hindu wedding ritual is extremely complex and is often performed under a *bedi*, or outdoor shrine. A priest, on behalf of the bride and groom, makes prayers and offerings, followed by ceremonial rituals, including four circlings around a sacred fire and the nuptial pole. Near the end of the ceremony, the priest ties the groom's sash to the bride's veil and the couple exchanges their wedding vows, which include these traditional Hindu phrasings from the ritual of Seven Steps:

We have taken the Seven Steps. You have become mine forever. Yes, we have become partners. I have become yours. Hereafter, I cannot live without you. Do not live without me. Let us share the joys. We are word and meaning, united. You are thought and I am sound. May the nights be honey-sweet for us; may the mornings be honey-sweet for us; may the earth be honey-sweet for us; may the heavens be honey-sweet for us. May the plants be honey-sweet for us; may the sun be all honey for us; may the cows yield us honey-sweet milk! As the heavens are stable, as the earth is stable, as the mountains are stable, as the whole universe is stable, so may our union be permanently settled.

Buddhist

The bride and groom's country of origin determines their wedding attire, as well as which cultural rituals are included as part of the ceremony.

A Buddhist ceremony may be held inside a Buddhist temple or outdoors. In either case, the actual ceremony takes place under a poruwa (a white silk canopy) which represents the couple's new home. The poruwa may be decorated with white flowers.

The officiant is an ordained clergy member, usually a monk. He may be addressed as "Reverend," "Lama," or "Roshi." The ceremony begins and ends with the ringing of bells. After the couple recites their vows and exchanges rings, the monk may perform a handfasting ceremony where he binds the hands of the couple with a silk sash or Buddhist rosary.

This is an example of a traditional Buddhist marriage homily:

In the future, happy occasions will come as surely as the morning. Difficult times will come as surely as night. When things go joyously, meditate according to the Buddhist tradition. When things go badly, meditate. Meditation is the manner of the Compassionate Buddha who will guide your life. To say the words 'love and compassion' is easy. But to accept that love and compassion are built upon patience and perseverance is not easy.

Wedding guests may be restricted in their attire, depending on the policies of each Buddhist temple. Call the temple prior to the wedding for guidance.

A man may be required to wear a jacket and tie; a woman may be expected to wear a dress or a skirt and blouse. Or, more casual attire may be acceptable. Also, according to proper etiquette, guests are not expected to bring gifts to the wedding.

Interfaith Ceremonies

An interfaith ceremony is one that combines elements of two different religious faiths. One of these ceremonies is complicated to plan because it involves locating an officiant who will agree to conduct such a ceremony, a religious venue that will allow it, and compromises on the part of the bride and groom.

The easiest way to understand the complexities involved in an interfaith ceremony is to use the example of a Jewish/Christian ceremony, one of the most common in the United States. Here are just a few of the problems they will encounter:

- When should we schedule our wedding? Christians often marry on a Saturday afternoon, but a Jew may never marry on the Sabbath.

- Will we need to find a nondenominational house of worship for the ceremony, or should we find a secular venue?

- A Christian believes in Jesus as the Messiah; a Jew does not.

- Which musical selection shall the bride choose to walk down the aisle? Although, a Christian bride usually chooses "Here Comes the Bride" by Wagner, a Jewish bride would not choose this selection because Wagner was an anti-Semitic.

- Will all the men be required to wear yarmulkes, because the groom is a Jew? The answer is that they can be designated as optional for an interfaith ceremony.

- Will the bride agree to omit "in Jesus' name" at the end of any ceremony prayers? Will she accept "in God's name" instead?

- How will the ceremony be divided between the two faiths? Will the rabbi and the priest decide?

- Traditionally, a Christian bride doesn't want her groom to see her before she walks down the aisle, but a Jewish bride and groom always see each other before the ceremony when they sign the ketubah.

- What type of pre-marital counseling will be required for an interfaith ceremony? Will you be required to agree to counseling by both the priest and the rabbi?

All your questions will be answered when you meet with the rabbi and the minister or priest. Interfaith ceremonies require compromises. For example, the ketubah may be signed *separately* by the bride and groom; that way the bride will fulfill the Jewish tradition of signing the ketubah before the ceremony, while still retaining the Christian tradition of not being seen by her groom until she walks down the aisle.

If either the bride or groom has a weaker allegiance to his or her faith, an interfaith ceremony is much easier to plan because one partner usually succumbs to the stronger partner's religious faith. So, for example, if the bride was raised Catholic as a child, but has not followed through with her faith as she became an adult, but the groom has strong Jewish beliefs, the bride may agree to a ceremony that is mostly Jewish, with a few Christian elements.

Typical division of elements in a Jewish/Christian ceremony

Rabbi

- Supervises the signing of an interfaith ketubah by the bride and groom before the beginning of the ceremony.
- Leads the blessing over the wine.
- Leads the Seven Wedding Blessings.
- Leads the exchange of vows and rings.
- Leads the breaking of the glass.
- Reads from the Torah.

Priest or minister

- Delivers opening blessing.
- Reads the Declaration of Consent.
- Reads from the New Testament.
- Conducts the unity candle ceremony.

Interfaith ceremonies are not allowed to take place within the walls of certain houses of worship. It is also difficult to find a religious officiant who will agree to conduct the ceremony. This is why many interfaith couples opt for a civil ceremony instead, especially in certain cases. For example, it's usually difficult to arrange a wedding in a Jewish synagogue between a Jewish and Christian couple, although some Jewish Reform rabbis will conduct the ceremony.

If you want an interfaith ceremony within the walls of a religious venue, you'll need to meet with several officiants until you find one who is liberal enough to sanction it. In some cases, a religious officiant may agree to preside over an interfaith ceremony if it's held at a secular venue. One of the best ways to find a rabbi who will officiate at an interfaith marriage is to ask around. If you know of another couple who was married by a rabbi at their interfaith ceremony, ask for a referral to that rabbi.

Once you've found a religious officiant from each of your faiths willing to participate in an interfaith ceremony, protocol requires that the officiant of the ceremony venue is the host and makes the final decisions on which faith's customs will be allowed. For example, you may want to include customs from each of your faiths, including musical selections, prayers, and Scripture readings.

Etiquette 101

It's considered in poor taste to plan an interfaith Jewish/Christian ceremony in a church where a cross is prominently displayed. Look for a nondenominational venue instead, such as a college chapel, an academic facility's venue, or a hotel or country club ballroom.

A sample Jewish/Christian interfaith order of service

Here's an example of how an interfaith Jewish-Christian ceremony may proceed:

- Opening remarks.
- Explanation of the chuppah.
- Memorializing loved ones who have died.
- Explaining the traditions of the two faiths.
- Blessing of the marriage.
- Prayer.

- Rabbi's, priest's, or minister's remarks.
- Ceremony readings.
- Blessing over the wine.
- Affirmation of the families and guests.
- Recitation of vows.
- Ring exchange(s).
- Unity candle ceremony.
- Seven Wedding Blessings.
- Pronouncement.
- Closing remarks and benediction.
- Breaking of the glass.

Examples of readings often used for an interfaith ceremony

I shall betroth you unto me forever,
I shall betroth you unto me in righteousness,
And in loving kindness and in compassion,
and I shall betroth you unto me in faithfulness.
(From the book of Hosea in the Bible)

I do not love you as if you were salt-rose, or topaz,
or the arrow of carnations the fire shoots off.
I love you as certain dark things are to be loved,
in secret, between the shadow and the soul.
I love you as the plant that never blooms
but carries in itself the light of hidden flowers;
thanks to your love a certain solid fragrance,
risen from the earth, lives darkly in my body.
I love you without knowing how, or when, or from where.
I love you straightforwardly, without complexities or pride;
so I love you because I know no other way
than this: where I does not exist, nor you,
so close that your hand on my chest is my hand,
so close that your eyes close as I fall asleep.
(Sonnet XVII, from *100 Love Sonnets* by Pablo Neruda)

If I have all the eloquence of men, women, or of angels, but speak without love, I am simply a gong booming or a cymbal clashing.

If I have the gift of prophecy, understanding all mysteries and knowing everything, and if I have all faith so as to move mountains, but am without love, I gain nothing.

If I give away all I possess, and if I deliver my body to be burned, but am without love, I gain nothing.

Love is always patient and kind; it is never jealous or selfish, it does not take offense and is not resentful.

Love takes no pleasure in other people's sins, but delights in the truth. It is always ready to excuse, to trust, and to endure whatever comes. Love does not end. There are in the end three things that last: Faith, Hope, and Love, and the greatest of these is Love.

(I Corinthians 12:31-13:8a)

Let there be spaces in your togetherness
And let the winds of heaven dance between you.
Love one another, but make not a bond of love:
Let it rather be a moving sea between the shores of your souls.
Sing and dance together and be joyous,
But let each one of you be alone,
Even as the strings of a lute are alone,
Though they quiver with the same music.
Give your hearts, but not into each other's keeping.
For only the hand of Life can contain your hearts,
And stand together yet not too near together:
For the pillars of the temple stand apart,
And the oak tree and the cypress grow not in each other's shadow.

(Excerpt from *The Prophet* by Kahlil Gibran)

Interfaith ceremony elements

The following are elements to consider adding to your interfaith ceremony.

The Agape Meal

An agape meal has been part of interfaith wedding ceremonies for many years. It is a sharing of bread and wine which symbolizes the couple's love for each other, and their promise to spread their love through the communities where they will live during their married life together.

Blessings for an interfaith marriage

The traditional Seven Blessings of the Jewish faith can be replaced with seven blessings that represent seven different cultures and religions. For example, if your family has an Irish heritage, you may include this traditional Irish wedding blessing:

May the road rise up to greet you.
May the wind be always at your back.
May the sun shine warm upon your face.
And until we meet again
May God hold you in the hollow of his hand.

Or, you may like this ancient Apache wedding blessing:

Now you will feel no rain,
for each of you will be shelter for the other.
Now there is no more loneliness,
for each of you will be companion to the other.
Now you are two persons,
but there is only one life before you.
Go now to your dwelling to enter into
the days of your togetherness.
And may your days be good,
and long upon the earth.

Finally, here is an ancient Gaelic wedding blessing:

Deep Peace of the running wave to you.
Deep Peace of the flowing air to you.
Deep Peace of the quiet earth to you.
Deep Peace of the shining stars to you.
Deep Peace of the spirit of peace to you.

Or, the blessings may be original blessings written and read by your friends and relatives.

The Circling

This is a lovely ritual often used in interfaith ceremonies. It comes from a Jewish tradition where the bride circles her groom three or seven times, symbolizing the times the Bible states, "When a man takes a wife." However, for an interfaith ceremony, the circling has a modern interpretation: it symbolizes the bride's and groom's marriage relationship where each becomes the center of the other's attention, and it symbolizes their respect for each other's religious faiths and their love for each other.

The bride and groom may circle each other only once, or choose the traditional circlings of three or seven times. Before each circles around the other, he or she recites the following from the book of Hosea in the Bible:

Bride/groom: *"I shall betroth thee unto me forever; Yes, I shall betroth thee unto me in righteousness, and in loving kindness and in compassion; and I shall betroth thee unto me in faithfulness."*

Readings of scripture appropriate for an interfaith ceremony

If the interfaith ceremony is Christian/Jewish, here are examples of Bible scriptures often included:

Old Testament scriptures, read by the rabbi

...wherever you go, I will go; wherever you lodge, I will lodge; your people shall be my people, and your God my God. (Ruth 1:16)

Wear me as a seal upon your heart
As a seal upon your arm;
For love is infinitely strong...
Many waters cannot quench love;
No flood can sweep it away. (Songs of Songs 8:6)

A time to be born, and a time to die;
a time to plant, and a time to pluck up what is planted;
a time to break down, and a time to build up;
a time to weep, and a time to laugh;
a time to cast away stones, and a time to gather stones together;
a time to embrace, and a time to refrain from embracing;
a time to seek, and a time to lose;
a time to keep, and a time to cast away;
a time to rend, and a time to sew;
a time to keep silence, and a time to speak;
a time to love, and a time to hate;
a time for war, and a time for peace.
(Ecclesiastes 3:1–8)

New Testament scriptures, read by the priest or minister

Let love be genuine; hate what is evil, hold fast to what is good. Love one another with affection... Rejoice in your hope, be patient in tribulation, be constant in prayer... (Romans 12:9–13)

Our God in heaven,
Hallowed be your name,
Your kingdom come,
Your will be done,
On earth as it is in heaven.
Give us today our daily bread.
And forgive us our trespasses,
As we forgive those
Who trespass against us,
And lead us not into temptation,
But deliver us from evil. Amen.
(The Lord's Prayer, Matthew 6:9–13)

In the beginning God made man and woman, male and female, and said, "For this reason a man shall leave his father and mother and be joined to his wife, and the two shall become one flesh." So they are no longer two, but one flesh. What therefore God has joined together, let no one put asunder. (Matthew 19:4–6)

Signing of an interfaith ketubah when the bride or groom is Jewish

Here is one example of an interfaith ketubah:

On the [day of the week], the [day] of [month], [year] (bride/groom), daughter/son of [parents' names], and (bride/groom), daughter/son of [parents' names], say: This ring symbolizes our free decision to create this ceremony which joins us and is prompted by the love that we have for each other. This love provides us with the determination to be ourselves, the capacity to surrender and the push to live life to its fullest. It gives us the courage to hope and the ability to make our dreams a reality. Our purpose in joining together is to nurture that love in each other and, as best we can, give it to others.

We promise to try to be ever open to one another while cherishing each other's uniqueness, to comfort and challenge each other through life's sorrow and joy, to share our intuition and insight with one another, and above all to do everything within our power to permit each other to become the person we are yet to be.

We also pledge to establish a home open to the spiritual potential in all life. A home wherein the flow of the seasons and the passages of life are celebrated through the symbols of our heritages. A home filled with reverence for learning, loving, and generosity. A home wherein ancient melody, candles and wine sanctify the table. A home joined ever more closely to the communities of the world.

A ketubah is signed by the bride, groom, and two witnesses; it is usually framed and hung in the couple's home after the wedding.

Popular interfaith wedding alternatives

Occasionally, an interfaith couple is unable to compromise when it comes to which elements should be included in an interfaith wedding ceremony. Consequently, they have *two* ceremonies, one for each of their religious faiths. For example, if a Jewish groom and a Baptist bride are marrying, they have two wedding ceremonies: a traditional Jewish wedding, conducted by a rabbi in a synagogue, followed by a traditional Baptist wedding, conducted by a pastor in the bride's church.

The advantage of two ceremonies is that the bride and groom are married according to the wedding traditions of their religious faiths. I know you're asking, "When are they considered 'officially' married?" The answer is that they are *legally* married during the first ceremony.

Alternatively, the bride and groom are legally married in a brief civil ceremony at the courthouse. Then, they are married at a unique interfaith ceremony of their own design that combines elements from both of their religious faiths. The bride and groom can designate any friend or family member to serve as an officiant. It isn't necessary for this person to be legally sanctioned to conduct a wedding ceremony in your state, because the couple is already legally married before the service begins. (Your friend or family member may be able to obtain a temporary license to legally marry you, in which case you won't need to go to the courthouse first.) The beauty of this idea is that the bride and groom write their own ceremony, including vows, readings, music, and other rudiments of their own choosing. No religious restrictions apply!

One of the biggest problems a couple faces when planning an interfaith wedding is their parents. The friction may begin as soon as the engagement is announced, and it accelerates from there, sometimes to the point where one of the sets of parents refuses to attend the wedding at all. If this should happen to you, be comforted by the fact that it is a common dilemma. Usually, the dissenting parents change their minds and decide to participate in the ceremony after all. If they don't, so be it.

Military Ceremony

A military ceremony usually takes place in a military chapel and is almost always considered a formal affair. The groom wears his dress uniform, as do any of his attendants who are also in the military. The groom may wear a sword. If so, the bride stands on his right. If not, she stands on his left. The men may not wear boutonnieres when in uniform.

The most stunning and dramatic part of a military wedding is when the bride and groom walk under arched military swords or rifles as they exit the chapel. Also, the wedding cake is usually cut using the groom's sword. The invitations must be worded properly (see Chapter 2).

If the bride is in the military, she may wear her dress uniform during the ceremony, or she may wear a traditional wedding gown.

|||||||||||||||||||||||||||||||||||||||||||||||||||||||||||||||||||||||||||||||||||||||||||||||||||||||||||

Etiquette 101

All guests who wear their military uniforms must be seated according to their rank, with the highest rank seated closer to the front.

|||||||||||||||||||||||||||||||||||||||||||||||||||||||||||||||||||||||||||||||||||||||||||||||||||||||||||

Double Ceremony

A double ceremony is one where two couples are married during the same service, usually two sisters or two brothers, or occasionally two cousins or close friends. This means there may be two groups of attendants and, of course, two brides and two grooms, so you'll need a ceremony venue large enough to hold all these people. Often, one group of attendants serves both couples.

In the case of two sisters being married in a double ceremony, the oldest sister walks down the aisle first and is the first to be married. The two couples stand at the altar at the same time; however, the oldest bride and her groom recite their wedding and ring vows first, followed by her younger sister and her groom.

||||||||||||||||||||||||||||||||||||||||||||||||||||||||||||||||||||||||||||||||||||||||||||||||||

What the Groom Needs to Know

Once you've met with your officiant, you'll know whether or not you and your bride are allowed to write your own vows. If you are, don't leave it until the last minute. Begin composing your vows now, even if only writing down words or phrases that come to mind. The more you collect your thoughts, the easier it will be to write them out in full later on.

||||||||||||||||||||||||||||||||||||||||||||||||||||||||||||||||||||||||||||||||||||||||||||||||||

Ceremony Music

A religious ceremony often has restrictions when it comes to ceremony music. If your particular faith or officiant allows musical selections of your choice, you'll find a selection of today's classic and contemporary favorites in Chapter 5.

Ceremony Flowers and Decorations

Flowers, along with your other ceremony venue decorations, will create a distinctive ambience for your big day. A good rule of thumb when it comes to wedding etiquette is that the more formal the wedding, the more profuse and elaborate the flowers should be. For example, for an ultraformal wedding, the bride usually carries an exquisite cascading bouquet, and the floral displays are elegant and oversized. Whereas, an informal wedding may only require a bridal corsage and one flower arrangement. Your wedding coordinator and/ or your florist or floral designer will offer suggestions that complement the theme and colors of your wedding.

The décor should be compatible with the formality of your wedding and the size and number of floral arrangements. The more formal the wedding, the more elaborate and upscale the decorations should be.

For example, an ultraformal wedding is usually decorated with genuine satin ribbons, as opposed to acetate ribbons which may be used for a less formal wedding. Also, a formal wedding may embellish the end of the pews with tall silver candle stands, decorated with satin bows and flowers. A less formal wedding may only require smaller acetate bows attached to the pews, and silk flowers may be substituted for fresh flowers. For an ultraformal or formal wedding, you might want to employ a floral designer instead of a regular florist.

A white aisle runner is often included in a formal or ultraformal ceremony. Some religions don't allow the use of an aisle runner. If you decide to use one, however, you need to practice unrolling it and walking on it during the wedding rehearsal. I've seen so many problems with aisle runners that I encourage couples to forget it. They sometimes bunch up, which can cause someone to trip, and rarely do they unroll evenly without some kind of problem.

Ceremony Photography and Videography

Most photographers restrict using a flash on their cameras during the ceremony itself, except when taking a photo of the bride as she enters the venue on her father's arm, and of the bride and groom as they exit the venue during the recessional. During the remainder of the ceremony, a photographer usually takes timed photos from the balcony or other inconspicuous spot.

The videographer may discretely record the entire ceremony. If the videographer has an assistant, two camcorders may be used, one from the rear of the venue and one from the front.

Many religious faiths do not allow any photography inside the religious venue.

IIIIIIIIIIIIIIIIIIIIIIIIIIIIIIIIIIIIIIIIIIIIIIIIIIIIIIIIIIIIIIIIIIIIIIIIIIIIIIIIIIIIIIIIIIIIIII

Etiquette 101

The bride should discourage having visitors in her dressing room before the ceremony. According to traditional etiquette, only the bride's attendants and the two mothers should be with her. Unfortunately, other friends and relatives feel they are special and have the right to stop by and wish the bride well before the ceremony. This is not the time for the bride to be welcoming guests. Being swamped with well-wishers is also dishonoring to the mothers who should be given the special privilege of being with the bride before the ceremony. My advice: lock the dressing room door!

IIIIIIIIIIIIIIIIIIIIIIIIIIIIIIIIIIIIIIIIIIIIIIIIIIIIIIIIIIIIIIIIIIIIIIIIIIIIIIIIIIIIIIIIIIIIIII

Ceremony Themes

Most ceremonies have some kind of theme. The theme may be simple or complex. In Chapter 5 you'll find themes suitable for an informal wedding; here you'll find lovely themes appropriate for a formal religious ceremony.

Victorian

A Victorian theme is nostalgic, romantic, and sentimental, with an abundance of lace, ribbons, hearts, and trailing ribbons. The bride and her attendants may wear Victorian-style gowns, including bustled skirts and high buttoned shoes. The bridesmaids may also carry lace parasols.

The bride may carry a tussy-mussy bouquet (a small cluster of flowers tied with ribbon or inserted into an elegant cone-shaped silver holder). Lace is incorporated into the bridesmaids' bouquets and floral decorations.

Indoor garden

Any indoor venue, including a home or a house of worship, can be converted into an exquisite garden. Consider using white or wrought iron benches, trellises, white wooden arbors, and picket fencing. Then add colorful flowering potted plants, shrubs, and trees, whether fresh or silk.

Snowball

This is a wedding where everyone wears white, including the mothers and grandmothers. The ribbons, flowers, and all other decorations are also white. The trick is for all the whites to be the same shade of white. Start with the most important purchase: the bride's gown. Then, using a sample of the gown's fabric as you shop, select your bridesmaids' gowns, mothers' and grandmothers' gowns, flowers, ribbon, and so on. A snowball wedding is stunning.

Christmas

A Christmas theme can be used for any wedding that takes place during the month of December. It's an easy theme to work with because Christmas trees, holly, poinsettias, candles, and evergreens are abundant during this month. It works best for an evening ceremony where tiny white lights have been strung around the venue to create a winter wonderland.

Black and white

This is a wedding where all the attire is black and white. The groomsmen wear black tuxedoes and the bridal attendants wear black gowns. The flower girl wears white and the ring bearer wears black. This is a popular theme, but be careful to splash a little color around the venue, in the ribbons or flowers; otherwise, the ceremony may lose its festive ambience.

Hearts and flowers

A hearts and flowers theme is appropriate for any time of year, but especially for a Valentine's Day wedding. This theme requires decorated hearts in all sizes, and an abundance of fresh and potted flowers. Wrap the pots or floral containers with crepe paper and ribbons in the wedding colors. The hearts can be cut from heavy poster board, covered with crepe paper, and edged with paper or ribbon lace ruffles. Large hearts may be hung on each side of the front of the venue, and smaller hearts may be used to embellish the pew decorations, candle sconces, candelabras, and floral arrangements. Tiny hearts may be attached to ribbons that trail down from the bride's and bridesmaids' bouquets.

Southern antebellum

Round up white picket fencing, a white arbor or gazebo, and as many fresh or silk magnolias, hydrangeas, or lilacs as you can find. The bride and her attendants may wear purchased or rented Southern belle gowns with hoop skirts and parasols. The men can wear white dinner jackets with black ties, trousers, and pin-striped vests. If it's an evening wedding, decorate the site with white candles and strings of tiny white lights.

Chapter 5

Civil Ceremonies

A civil ceremony, also known as a legal ceremony, may be held at a government office, such as the judge's chambers, or at a secular venue, such as a resort, country club, private home, or other secular site. It's usually officiated by a judge, justice of the peace, or other court official who is allowed to conduct a legally binding wedding in your state. In some states, you are allowed to have a friend or relative receive a temporary permit to conduct your civil ceremony.

It should be noted that just because a couple chooses to have a civil ceremony, instead of a religious ceremony, doesn't mean that they're not religious. In our children's cases, our daughter had a religious ceremony in a church, and our son had a civil ceremony at a golf resort. However, our son's ceremony was just as meaningful as our daughter's. The biggest difference was that our son and his fiancée had complete control of their ceremony, with no restrictions. The officiant for our son's wedding was a personal friend who happened to be a judge, legally qualified to perform marriages in the state of California.

When a couple chooses a civil ceremony, they have the option of including any religious elements they desire. In fact, they have complete total control over their ceremony, which gives them the freedom to be as creative as they want as they make their plans. Here are a few reasons why couples opt for a civil ceremony:

- The couple has the freedom to choose a formal or informal ceremony venue, such as an upscale resort or their parents' back yard. They may even opt for a super-casual site, such as a beach or a city park. No rules apply.

- A civil ceremony is the perfect option for the couple planning an interfaith wedding, because there are no religious complications or restrictions.

- The couple may include their own choice of music, readings, and order of service.

- They are free to write their own original wedding vows.

- They are free to personalize their wedding with any of the special touches, such as those described in Chapter 7.

- Their wedding reception may be personalized as well, with no etiquette requirements, such as a formal ceremony must be followed by a formal reception. However, if the couple *prefers* a formal reception following their informal civil ceremony, that's fine.

Original Wedding Vows

If you decide to write your own vows, here are several couples' original vows to inspire you:

I bring myself to you this day to share my life with you; you can trust my love, for it's real. I promise to be a faithful mate and to unfailingly share and support your hopes, dreams, and goals. I vow to be there for you always. When you fall, I will catch you. When you cry, I will comfort you. When you laugh, I will share your joy. Everything I am and everything I have is yours, from this moment forth and for eternity.

[Bride/groom's name], you are God's precious gift to me. You are my spring-time, my hope and my joy. You are everything that's good, pure, and true, and I worship you with my mind, body, and soul. How blessed I am to be able to say that you are mine, to be able to love and cherish you for the rest of my life. I vow to be a good husband/wife to you, [bride/groom's name], always putting you first in my life, always there to comfort you in your sorrow, and rejoice with you in your victories. May our hearts and breath become one as we unite this day as husband and wife. I promise to be your true love from this day forward.

[Bride/groom's name], ever since you came into my life, my days have been bright and glorious, but today, our wedding day, is the brightest of them all, a golden moment, made splendid by our love for each other. And yet, this beautiful moment is only a taste of what is to come as we share our lives together. I pledge

my love to you. I promise to be faithful and true to you, and I rejoice in my good fortune to have found you as my mate.

[Bride/groom's name], I searched for you all my life, looking for you, watching for you, needing you, wanting you, but I didn't know who you were until God brought you to me. Your love has touched my heart. [bride/groom's name], you alone are the love of my life, my dream come true. Now that I've found you, I feel that I've known you always, my soul mate, my precious bride/groom. I was only half a person until you came into my life, but now I am whole and complete. How I love and adore you,[bride/groom's name], and I give myself to you this day with complete joy and abandonment. I promise to be a true and faithful husband/wife, to comfort you, honor you, respect you, and cherish you for all our days together on this earth.

Until I met you, marriage-type love was an abstract thing I only read about in poems, heard sung in romantic love songs, or read about in books. But when I met you I knew for the first time what it was to experience this type of love within my heart. You have made me a believer in the real thing, in the promise of a love that will last a lifetime. There is nothing more important to me than your love. I value it above money, power, or position. I rejoice in our love, and I promise to walk by your side with a constancy that only comes from unreserved commitment, and it is this commitment I make to you now as I take you as my husband/wife, from this day forward and for as long as we both shall live.

I come to you today just as I am, and I take you just as you are, my cherished husband/wife. Let's never change, but always love each other the way we do today, the man and woman we are as we stand here before these witnesses and commit ourselves to each other for life.

[Bride/groom's name], it takes a great amount of trust to pledge oneself to another for a lifetime. I do that now as I affirm you as my soul mate, my life partner. I will be your dearest friend, your love, and the father/mother of your children. I accept you, [bride/groom's name], as my husband/wife, and I pledge myself to you without reservation.

I take you, [bride/groom's name], as my adored and cherished husband/wife. I promise to be a loving and faithful husband/wife. May our sunshine be shared, our rain be gentle, and our sweet love eternal. I pledge myself to you from this day forward and for all eternity.

Bride: *I promise, before our family and friends, to be your true, faithful, and loving wife.*

Groom: *And I promise, before our family and friends, to be your true, faithful, and loving husband.*

Bride: *I will do everything in my power to keep our love as fresh and strong as it is today.*

Groom: *And I will be true to you, with my body and my mind, always putting you first in my life.*

Bride: *Your love has changed my life, and I'm a better person because of you.*

Groom: *Your faith in me has given me a new confidence and an unexplainable joy.*

Bride: *I thank God for you and I pledge my love to you from this day forward.*

Groom: *And I will love you always. This is my pledge.*

Additional vows can be found in chapters 4, 6, and 7.

Original Ring Vows

Here are some vows that can be recited during the exchanging of rings:

When we were in high school, I gave you my class ring and you wore it on a chain around your neck, to show everyone that we were going steady. But today I give you something much more precious: a wedding ring. May it be a sign to all who see it that you belong to me alone, and that we're going steady for the rest of our lives.

You are my life, my love, my best friend, and with this ring I wed thee; may it be a reminder of my love and the sacred commitment I have made here today.

Today we're on a mountaintop; everything is good and happy and right. But someday there will be valleys as well, and as we walk through those valleys together, may this ring be a reminder of this mountaintop experience, and the vows we have made this day.

Music

A civil ceremony at a secular site will have few, if any, restrictions when it comes to music. You may include any of the classic or contemporary selections listed below, or you are free to include your favorites from today's pop charts. Before and during your engagement period, you may have adopted a certain song as "our song." If you have a special piece of music, feel free to include it in your civil ceremony, as long as the song is tasteful and appropriate for a wedding.

Prelude music
- Adagio from Sonata in E-flat (Mozart)
- Air from Water Music (Handel)
- Arioso (Bach)
- Canon in D (Pachelbel)
- Claire de Lune (Debussy)
- Larghetto (Handel)
- Moonlight Sonata (Beethoven)
- "O Perfect Love" (Burleigh)
- Prelude to the Afternoon of a Faun (Debussy)
- "The Wedding Song" (Stuckey)
- "Three Times a Lady" (Ritchie)
- "Trumpet Tune" (Purcell)

Processional/recessional music
- Aria in F Major (Handel)
- Bridal Chorus from Lohengrin (Wagner)
- Fanfare, Te Deum (Charpentier)
- Jesu, Joy of Man's Desiring (Bach)
- March in C (Purcell)
- Ode to Joy (Beethoven)
- Royal Fireworks Music (Handel)
- Sheep May Safely Graze (Bach)
- Spring, The Four Seasons (Vivaldi)
- Trumpet Voluntary (Clarke)

- Wedding March from *A Midsummer Night's Dream* (Mendelssohn)
- "Wedding Processional" from *The Sound of Music* (Rogers)
- "You are the Sunshine of My Life" (Stevie Wonder)

Ceremony music

- "All I Ask of You" (from *The Phantom of the Opera*, Webber, Hart, and Stilgoe)
- "Flesh of My Flesh" (Patillo)
- "God Gave Me You" (Kaiser)
- "Grow Old With Me" (Carpenter)
- "Hawaiian Wedding Song" (Hoffman and Manning)
- "O Perfect Love" (Barnby)
- "The Bridal Prayer" (Copeland)
- "The Greatest of These is Love" (Bitgood)
- "The Wedding Song" (Stuckey)
- "Two Candles" (Salsbury)
- "What I Did for Love" (Hamlisch)
- "Whither Thou Goest, I Will Go" (Martin)

If you have a certain musical selection you want included, but the musicians aren't familiar with it, purchase the sheet music and provide it for them.

Contemporary Alternatives to a Traditional Wedding

The traditional wedding ceremony and reception are often replaced by a contemporary alternative, such as a surprise wedding, weekend wedding, all-night wedding, or a super-casual wedding. Another popular alternative is a destination wedding (see Chapter 10). These weddings are less expensive, more convenient, and, often, more practical for their families. After all, a lot of couples "just want to get married" and don't have the time, money, and energy to plan a large traditional wedding.

Surprise wedding

A surprise wedding is a clever idea because it takes place during a separate event that has already been planned, such as a family reunion, a holiday get-together, a New Year's Eve party, or any other social event where friends and family already plan to attend.

By "surprise wedding," I don't mean that it's a surprise to the bride and groom—only to those in attendance. Of course, the officiant must be in on the surprise, because without him or her, there won't be a wedding.

Weekend wedding

The trendy weekend wedding is one part family reunion, one part vacation, and one part wedding. Usually, the weekend begins with a Friday evening get-together hosted by a family member, which includes a cocktail welcome party, wedding rehearsal, and the rehearsal dinner. The guests are entertained during the day on Saturday with a barbecue picnic, a poolside party, or sports activities, such as golf tournaments and tennis matches.

The wedding and reception are held on Saturday evening, followed by a full day of activities for the guests on Sunday, including such things as a brunch or a sightseeing tour around the city.

All-night wedding

An all-night wedding is exactly what it says: a wedding that lasts all night long, finally ending with breakfast. It takes place at a hotel or resort and evolves quickly into a party, with eating, drinking, and dancing throughout the night, although some of the guests may crash for a while in a suite of rooms that have been reserved for them.

When refreshed, they wake up, drink a little coffee, and keep going. This type of wedding celebration is perfect for a New Years Eve wedding, with the ceremony taking place around 11 p.m., followed by cocktails and hors d'oeuvres until midnight when the party begins.

Super-casual wedding

This is a wedding perfectly suited for the couple who wants something affordable and uncomplicated. It may take place on a beach, at the top of a ski slope, in a hot air balloon, or at any other unique venue. The reason this has become a popular choice for today's brides and grooms is that it's a simple wedding, where they are surrounded only by their closest friends and family members.

Ceremony Themes for an Informal Wedding

Choosing a theme for an informal wedding is optional, especially if the ceremony takes place on the shore of a lake where Mother Nature has already provided all the ambience you'll need. If you would like a more complex theme for your informal wedding, here are a few ideas:

Renaissance

Renaissance weddings are enormously popular, but you should know that one of these weddings is not only complicated to plan, but more expensive than an average wedding. You can give any setting a Renaissance ambience, although certain settings work best, such as an historic castle, on a farm, or in an open field.

Traditional Renaissance wedding attire is the most important element. The bride may wear a traditional ball gown with bell shaped sleeves, and her attendants may wear flowing gowns with pointy hats or flowered wreaths on their heads. The men usually wear velvet doublets, shirts with billowing sleeves, and feathered hats. The groom wears a sword at his side.

For more ideas, attend a Renaissance festival or research online at such sites as *www.renaissancefestival.com.*

Polynesian

Guests love a Polynesian wedding theme because it reminds them of happy, carefree vacations spent in Hawaii. It works best around water, such as a swimming pool, a beach, or on the banks of a lake or river, although an indoor venue will work as well.

If outdoors, decorate with tiki torches. If indoors, use conch shells and colorful fresh or silk flowers. The bride and groom wear traditional Hawaiian wedding attire, the bridesmaids wear colorful Hawaiian print gowns, and the groomsmen may wear white slacks and flowered Hawaiian shirts. Every member of the wedding party wears a fresh orchid lei, and each guest is presented with a silk or fresh orchid lei upon arrival.

Include the "Hawaiian Wedding Song" in your ceremony, plus any other Hawaiian favorites, especially during the prelude candle lighting ceremony and the lighting of the unity candle.

Country western

This theme calls for an informal venue, such as a barn or a ranch. The site is decorated with all things country western: lariats, cowboy hats, bales of hay, and, if you're lucky, you might find a hay wagon to use as transportation. Everyone dresses in western garb, including the bride, groom, all members of the wedding party, and the guests.

Other themes

You can personalize your ceremony venue with any theme you can think up, whether it's been done before or not. For example, you and your fiancé may be totally into square dancing, or perhaps you're devoted NASCAR fans. Whatever your interests, you can incorporate them into your wedding theme. Some ideas include:

- Autumn harvest.
- Fourth of July.
- Indy 500.
- Ice palace.
- Mexican fiesta.
- Oktoberfest.
- Classic cars.
- Halloween.
- Beach party.
- Tropical rain forest.
- Hollywood movie.

Chapter 6

Encore Ceremonies

In this chapter we'll talk about two types of encore ceremonies, second marriage ceremonies and vow renewal ceremonies.

Second Marriage Ceremonies

A second marriage is where the bride, groom, or both have been married before. Many of these wedding ceremonies include their children, who serve as members of their wedding party or are involved in some other way. Thirty percent of weddings today are second marriages.

The ceremony may be large or small, elaborate or modest. If this is a first marriage for one of you, you may decide to have a full-blown affair. These are some elements often found in a second wedding:

- Usually smaller and less elaborate than the first.
- Great emphasis on the importance and sanctity of their commitment to each other.
- Total cost is about half of a first wedding.
- The couple spends more on the honeymoon than first-time couples.
- If the first marriage ended in pain or bitterness, the bride or groom wants this ceremony to be as different as possible from their first.
- If this is the bride's second marriage, she may wear any color gown, including white; however, the gown will usually not have a long train, and the veil (if there is one) does not cover her face.

- Bride and groom write their own personalized vows.
- Personalized vows often mention children from previous marriages.
- The children are also included in the wedding party.

If only one of you was married before, be sensitive to the desires of the first-time bride or groom. Even though it may be a bride's second marriage, for example, her groom may have his heart set on a traditional ceremony and reception, so talk things over before you make any major planning decisions.

Even though you and your fiancé have plenty of worldly goods left over from your first marriages and you don't want your guests to feel obligated to buy wedding gifts, it's considered poor taste to say so. In fact, go ahead and establish gift registries, although you'll probably want to register for less traditional gifts, such as camping gear or artwork from a gallery. Do *not* print "No gifts please" at the bottom of your wedding invitations—a mega no-no.

If a friend or relative would like to host a bridal shower or co-ed party for you, that's fine. However, if the bride's friends and family members already hosted several bridal showers the first time around, they shouldn't be expected to do so again. If they want to host an engagement party, that would be in good taste.

Invite anyone you'd like to your wedding, whether they were guests at your first wedding or not, although it's usually best not to invite your ex to your wedding, especially if your ex is the parent of your children. If your ex is in attendance, that can be confusing to your children, who are getting used to being part of a new family unit. If you have a sweet relationship with your former in-laws, and they are supportive of your new marriage, you may want them at your wedding, whether your ex is there or not. Introduce them as your children's grandparents. Do not introduce them as, "My former mother-in-law" and so on.

When an encore couple announces their engagement, this is the order in which it should be made: your children, your ex-spouse, your parents, your relatives and friends, in your local newspaper.

If either of you has children from a previous marriage, it's important to tell them first. The worst thing that can happen is for them to hear the news from someone else. Your children may feel threatened by this news, fearing they'll lose your love and be relegated to second place in your life, so reassure them of your love. Follow up your announcement with exciting ways you plan to include them in your wedding. Tell each child separately, one after the other, on the same day. You don't want one of your children telling a sibling before you've had a chance to do so. If—heaven forbid!—your children don't approve of your engagement, hope and pray your fiancé wins them over before the wedding. If this doesn't happen, don't hesitate to schedule a few sessions with a marriage and family counselor, who may be able to help. By the way, one way to perk of their interest is to plan a two-phase honeymoon: The first phase is your private honeymoon, just the two of you. The second phase includes your kids. For example, make it a family "honeymoon" at Disneyland.

The next person to be informed is your ex-spouse, particularly if he or she is the parent of your children. If you had no children together, it's still a good idea for the ex-spouse to hear the news from you instead of from someone else. Also, if possible, tell your ex in person and in private—not in front of your children.

Tell each set of parents separately, and in person. Your fiancé should tell his parents, and you should do likewise.

As for your other relatives and friends, tell them in person or with a telephone call. If you can't reach all of them within a reasonable length of time, send notes. Your goal is to be sure they all hear the news within the same general time frame.

You may announce your own engagement, or your parents may do so. It will depend on who will be hosting the wedding. Because most encore weddings are planned and paid for by the couple themselves, you'll probably announce your own engagement. If there are children from previous marriages, they may be included in the announcement. They may also be mentioned as being members of your wedding party. For example, your daughter may serve as flower girl and your fiancé's son may serve as ring bearer. If your children are older, they may serve as your honor attendants. Here is sample wording when the couple and their children announce their engagement together:

> *Estelle Anne Jameson and Thomas Robert Edmonds,*
> *along with their children, Bianca, Joel, and Patrice,*
> *announce their engagement to marry (etc.)*

Original wedding vows for a second marriage

Here are some samples of wedding vows for your second wedding:

[Bride/groom's name], you are my new day, a beautiful ray of light that broke through the darkness of my despair. Thank you for your smile, your sense of humor, and your loving spirit. I promise to love you and cherish you all the days of my life.

I, [groom's name], take you [bride's name] as my lawfully wedded wife. I promise to love you and be true to you in sickness and in health, in good times and bad, always putting you first in my life. I thank the Lord for rescuing me from my despair by sending you to me, my cherished treasure, His most precious and undeserved gift.

[Groom's name], you are my healer, my comforter, and the joy of my life. Your love has restored my torn, broken heart. Your smile has healed my pain, and your caring spirit has rescued mine from the dark places. I love you, [groom's name], and I vow to be a faithful, loving husband/wife, to care for you, comfort you, and cherish you for as long as we both shall live.

[Bride's name], I am proud to marry you this day and become your husband/ wife. I promise to wipe away your tears with my laughter, and your pain with my caring and compassion. We will wipe clean the old canvas of our lives, and let God, with His amazing artistic talent, fill it with new color and beauty. I give myself to you completely as your husband/wife, and I promise to love you always.

When I first met you, [bride's name], I was drawn to you immediately, but I was resigned never to marry again, after the pain I had suffered through the years. But your love was so tender and genuine, so compassionate and caring, until you crept slowly into my life. Inch by inch you permeated my being, as your love fell softly onto my heart. You have turned my life around. Because of your love, each day is a new delight, a new awakening. My heart belongs to you, dear [bride's name], and I pledge here today in the presence of our friends and family, to be your faithful husband/wife, to stand beside you, upholding you, cherishing you for the rest of our lives.

Ways to include your children in the ceremony

Your children should feel part of the ceremony, so much so that in years to come they will remember this as the "day we got married." Here are several touching ways you can include your children:

- Serving as a member of the wedding party, as best man, maid of honor, flower girl, ring bearer, bell-ringer, candle lighter, or usher.
- Walking you down the aisle.
- Reading a poem or special verse.
- Handing out ceremony programs.
- Singing a song.
- Playing a musical instrument.

Order flowers for all your children, including a boutonniere for your young son or a small wrist corsage for your young daughter.

When you're planning the seating arrangements for your reception, dedicate a special table for your children and a few of their cousins or friends who may be in attendance. Decorate their table in some unique way, with personalized balloons, or special favors at each place setting.

Family unity candle ceremony

A traditional unity candle ceremony consists of the lighting of a central candle from two separate candles held by the bride and groom, symbolizing the uniting of two lives into one. A family unity candle ceremony is similar, except there are additional candles—one for each child. So, the bride, groom, and each child lights the central unity candle at the same time, symbolizing they have formed a new family unit, unified as one. A variation of this is for the bride and her children to hold one candle, and the groom and his children to hold the other candle. These two candles are used to light the unity candle at the same time. Another poignant variation is for the bride and groom to light the unity candle from their respective candles, then light their children's candles from the wick of the unity candle.

Family medallion ceremony

The family medallion is a beautiful round medal that has three intertwined circles, symbolizing family, love, and unity. The first two circles represent the union of the man and woman, and the third circle represents the children who are intertwined within their love. The medal is placed on a gold or sterling silver chain, forming a necklace which is placed over each child's neck, following the couple's wedding vows.

As the parents place the medallions over the necks of their children, they pledge to love and support their children as they become part of their family unit.

The bride and groom each pledge this vow to the children:

[The first names of their children], today we have become husband and wife, but we have also become a precious new family. I promise to be the best father [or mother] I can possibly be, as I care for you, protect you, support you, and love you with all my heart, for all the days of my life.

Circle of acceptance ceremony

This is a sweet ceremony that takes place in front of the altar. You, your children, and the officiant stand in a circle and hold hands. The officiant addresses each child, saying something like this:

Officiant: *[Child's name], your mommy and your new daddy want you to feel accepted into your new family being formed today. They also want your blessing. Do you, Cindy, accept your new family circle?*

Child: *Yes.*

Congregational blessing

Children are often included as part of the congregational blessing upon the bride, groom, and their child or children.

Minister (to the congregation): *Will you lend your hearts and concerns to this couple and their children, upholding them in prayer and encouraging them in their new life together?*

Congregation: *We will.*

Rose ceremony

As part of a rose ceremony (see Chapter 7), the bride and groom present a rose to the other's child. For example, the bride may present a rose to her groom's son, and the groom may present a rose to his bride's daughter.

Children included in your vows

Sixty-four percent of second marriages involve their children from previous marriages, so it's easy to see why they're being included in the couple's personalized vows. Here are examples:

Officiant (addressing the groom or bride, referring to the child): *And do you, [groom or bride's name], take [child's name] as your own, promising to love her and care for her, providing for her needs, physical and spiritual?*

Groom or bride: *I do.*

Officiant (addressing the child): *And do you, [child's name], take [groom or bride's name], to be your loving father [or mother] from this day forward?*

Child: *I do.*

Groom or bride (addressing the child): *[Child's name], I place this ring on your finger as a sign of my loving promise made this day.*

Groom: *Not only do I vow to be a good and faithful husband to you, [bride's name], but I also vow to be a patient, loving father to [children's names], caring for them and providing for them as my own. I vow to be their strength and their emotional support, loving them with all my heart from this day forward.*

Groom: *[Child's name], I love your Mommy, and today I have taken her to be my wife, but did you know that I love you dearly as well? I want to be as a father to you, and I invite you into my heart. We will have happy times together, you and your Mommy and I. And with this ring I give you my love.* (Slides a ring onto the girl's finger.)

The bride may recite the same vow to her new stepson. The bride or groom may choose a bracelet or necklace instead of a ring.

|||||||||||||||||||||||||||||||||||||||||||||||||||||||||||||||||||||||||||||||||||||||||||||||||||||||||

Etiquette 101

When the officiant pronounces you man and wife, include your children by having them stand beside you during the announcement. You want your children to remember this day as the "day we got married," so the officiant may add, "I would also like to introduce Jennifer and Jeffrey, part of this beautiful new family created today."

|||||||||||||||||||||||||||||||||||||||||||||||||||||||||||||||||||||||||||||||||||||||||||||||||||||||||

Second Wedding Toasts

The following are toasts that may be used at a second wedding.

A toast for the bride and groom

I would like to propose a toast to our newlyweds. This day is especially precious because you are so blessed to be given a second chance at happiness. What a wonderful day of renewed hope and joy. It is a day of peace and contentment—a sweet calm after a cold, fearsome storm. I can speak for everyone in this room when I say that we wish you all the happiness you deserve. We are so glad you found each other, and, just remember, the best is yet to come. Here's to [bride's name] and [groom's name].

A toast by the bride to her groom, or by the groom to his bride

Today I have married my best friend, my lifesaver, my healer, my sweetheart. Before I met you, [bride or groom's name], I was only half a person, a broken man [or woman]. But your love has fallen softly on my heart and made me whole again. You are the most compassionate, tender, caring person I've ever known. To our future!

A toast for the bride and groom and to their children from a previous marriage

I would like to propose a toast to [bride's name] and [groom's name] and [children's names]. What a beautiful picture you make as you stand together as a new little family. I speak for everyone in this room when I tell you how happy we are for all of you, and we wish you all the happiness you deserve. God bless you, and go with our congratulations and best wishes for a wonderful future. Here's to you all.

A toast from the bride or groom to their children

I would like to propose a toast to my beautiful daughter, [child's name]. You look so pretty today, and I'm so proud to be your father/mother. Thank you for being so loving and sweet, and for welcoming [bride or groom's name] into our family. We're going to have fun times together. I love you!

To my handsome son, [child's name]. Thank you for standing beside me today as my best man. I'm so proud of you and thankful to you for loving [bride's name] and welcoming her into our family. To [child's name], I love you.

Etiquette 101

The bride should not wear her engagement ring until any pending divorces are final. She may wear the ring on a chain around her neck or under her clothing, until the coast is clear.

Vow Renewal Ceremonies

A vow renewal ceremony is for the couple who wants to celebrate their years of marriage by renewing their vows during a wedding ceremony. It is also a strengthening of their marriage commitment. By the time a couple has been married 10, 25, 40, or even 50 years, they have survived myriad crises. This has fortified their deep love for each other. The trend is for these ceremonies to resemble a regular wedding ceremony, complete with bridesmaids, groomsmen, flowers, decorations, music, readings, and an officiant to "marry them" again. A vow renewal ceremony is usually hosted by the couple or the couple's children.

For both ceremony and reception, the degree of formality and choice of venues is similar to those of any wedding, ranging from a ultraformal cathedral wedding to a casual one on the beach. Does your house of worship or senior center conduct group renewal ceremonies? If so, your ceremony can take place as part of the group, followed by a private wedding reception of your choice.

By the way, if the idea of a vow renewal ceremony is appealing but the planning is not, hire a party planner or wedding coordinator to take care of all the details.

Choice of officiant

You may choose a religious officiant, such as your rabbi, priest, or minister, or a friend or family member may conduct the ceremony. Because the officiant does not need to be legally sanctioned to conduct a marriage ceremony, you may choose anyone you would like. You'll need to furnish him or her with the proper words to say, but that shouldn't be a problem. Take a look in Chapter 4 for officiant's words usually spoken during a wedding ceremony.

Popular vow renewal wedding venues

The following are venues often used for a vow renewal.

A church or chapel

The trend is toward full-blown weddings that include members of the wedding party, along with a facsimile of your original wedding ceremony. Take a look at your original wedding photos and try to duplicate the bridal bouquet, altar arrangements, pew decorations, music, and all the other elements included in your wedding. If you included a unity candle ceremony in your first wedding, incorporate it into your renewal ceremony.

At the reception, follow through with a similar wedding meal, wedding cake, favors, plus a toast by your best man, and so on.

On the beach

Plan a romantic renewal ceremony on the beach, Polynesian style. Everyone wears a fresh flower lei, including the bride and groom. The bride and groom wear white embroidered wedding tops and white slacks, while the guests wear white shorts or slacks with colorful Hawaiian shirts. After the ceremony, everyone strolls barefoot along the beach to the lilt of ukuleles and the Hawaiian Wedding Song. You don't need a Hawaiian beach to pull this off; any beach will do, whether it's on the ocean, a riverbank, or beside a picturesque lake.

A mountain setting

If you love the outdoors, you'll find romantic venues in the mountains. For example, if you're planning a summer ceremony, how about a mountain meadow lined with aspen trees? Or along a mountain stream or lake? If you're planning a winter ceremony, reserve a section of the lodge's dining room for your celebration. Then make your getaway on cross-country skis to your private cabin in the trees.

A city park

How about an old-fashioned picnic in the park? Decorate with streamers and helium balloons. Set a festive table, complete with an informal wedding cake, such as a cake that depicts the couple's favorite hobbies. Make it a pot-luck affair, and you'll have a meaningful, yet affordable, celebration.

Resort or country club ballroom

Set up the room to resemble a small chapel, complete with white chairs, "pew" bows, floral arrangements, an "altar," music, plus an officiant to conduct the ceremony. After your vows have been renewed, treat your guests to a decadent dessert and champagne reception.

A private room at an upscale restaurant

Arrange to have your renewal ceremony before Sunday brunch is served. Everyone helps themselves to brunch, which is eaten in your private venue where your wedding cake is on display. Of course, after you cut your cake, the toasts and champagne will flow.

An at-home ceremony

Depending on the size of your guest list, the ceremony can take place in the largest room of your home. If you have a lovely staircase, descend from it as a CD plays the wedding march. A home can be decorated for a wedding in an amazing way—the key is to remove as much furniture as possible, plus all clutter. Give the venue an elegant, spacious ambience with flowers, ribbons, candles, and lovely music. Your dining room table can serve your wedding buffet meal and wedding cake.

A private garden

Whether your backyard or a relative's incredible rose garden, host an informal wedding and reception. Designate a spot for the vow renewal, perhaps in front of a decorated arch or flowering trellis. The wedding feast can be as simple as barbecued ribs or chicken, along with favorite family side dishes. A wedding cake is required, however, in spite of the informal setting. If your backyard is a bit drab at the moment, make a trip to Home Depot and purchase pots filled with blooming plants and flowers. Wrap the ugly pots with crepe paper of your choice, tie with ribbons, and soon your garden will be filled with color.

Types of surprise ceremonies

There are three types of surprise vow renewals: ones planned by the couple's children, those planed by a husband for his wife, or ones that are a part of a family vacation.

Planned by the couple's children

As a gift to their parents, the children plan a surprise ceremony. It may take place during their parents' wedding anniversary celebration, during a family holiday get-together, or any other time of year. This surprise ceremony is a loving way for the children to honor their parents. The ceremony may be simple or complex. If a simple ceremony, only two elements are required: renewal of their vows and a lovely wedding cake for them to cut together.

Planned by the husband for his wife

There is a trend for the husband to plan a surprise vow renewal celebration as a gift to his wife. The planning will involve everything including choosing the venue, the menu, and the wedding cake; ordering flowers and champagne; and inviting the guests. The wife thinks they're going out for their anniversary to an upscale restaurant. What an awesome surprise!

Planned by the couple as part of a family vacation

Plan a family vacation, whether at your family's traditional getaway venue or a tropical island or a family cruise. Make arrangements ahead of time so that everything is ready for the surprise: a private spot where you can renew your vows, eat a wedding feast, cut your wedding cake, and drink champagne. The ceremony can be as elaborate as you like by including flowers, music, readings, and any other elements typically part of a wedding ceremony.

Many destination resorts and cruise lines offer vow renewal wedding packages, including such things as massages on the beach or a getaway ride on a pair of elegant white horses who carry you off into the sunset. On a cruise, your ceremony will be officiated by the ship's captain, either on deck, in a formal dining room, or in the ship's chapel. One of these packages often includes champagne, commemorative champagne flutes, a bouquet, boutonniere, and a three-tiered wedding cake. Live or recorded music is also furnished, along with a photographer and videographer.

|||||||||||||||||||||||||||||||||||||||||||||||||||||||||||||||||||||||||||||||||||||||||||||||||||||||

Etiquette 101

It's considered poor etiquette to register for gifts for a vow renewal ceremony.

|||||||||||||||||||||||||||||||||||||||||||||||||||||||||||||||||||||||||||||||||||||||||||||||||||||||

Reaffirmation wedding vows

A simple way to handle the vows at a reaffirmation ceremony is for the minister to read their original vows that were recited at their original wedding ceremony, then ask the couple if they do freely reaffirm those vows.

The officiant may ask, after reading their original vows: *Remembering these vows, made so many years ago on [date], do you now reaffirm these vows and your pledge of love and fidelity for each other?*

The couple answers: *I do.*

The couple then recites their original ring vows as they each place a ring on their mate's finger.

Other couples want a "new and improved" wedding ceremony, which they plan with care, including personalized vows. Here are examples of personalized renewal vows and ring vows:

I thank God, our heavenly Father, for bringing us together to love and care for each other. Every year, as we have walked through our days together, whether joyous or difficult, I thanked God to have you by my side. You have always been there for me, [husband or wife's name], filled with love, understanding, and encouragement, freely offering a smile and a hug. Today as we reaffirm our wedding vows, I commit my life to you anew and I vow to be a loving, true and faithful husband as long as we both shall live.

|||||||||||||||||||||||||||||||||||||||||||||||||||||||||||||||||||||||

[Husband or wife's name] ours has been a fairy-tale love story. From that first day we met until this very moment, our love has been one to be envied. We have been partners who grew more and more in love each day as we journeyed through life together. Our children have been the fruit of our love, and our grandchildren as well. We have a lifetime of shared memories, shared joys, shared sorrows, and our love has soared above it all. Today, as we renew our wedding vows before our beloved friends and family, I do so as an expression of how much I love and adore you. Ours is a love story destined to last until death do us part.

As we stand here today, renewing our wedding vows, I recall our wedding day so well. We were so young, so hopeful, so full of dreams. And most of our dreams have come true. But not all. And the disappointments hurt more than we thought they would, didn't they? And yet, our good times were even better than we expected. If I could have known then, what I know now, would I have married you? Yes, most certainly; with the same joy and commitment I feel today; as I promise to be your devoted and faithful husband/wife for the years we have left together in this life.

You are still my bride, my precious one, as beautiful and lovely as the day I married you. You are the most important person in my life, and I intend to keep it that way. Our marriage has succeeded, while so many have failed, because we have kept the laughter and thrown out the pain. Although we have winked at life, and laughed at its transient problems, we have always taken our marriage seriously. Yes, marriage is a fragile thing, and one that has lasted as long as ours is a precious rarity, to be held carefully and cherished forever. As we celebrate our [number] anniversary today, in the presence of these witnesses, I hereby reaffirm my vows, to love you, comfort you, honor and keep you, in sickness and in health, in sorrow and in joy, and to be faithful to you as long as we both shall live.

[Number] years ago, I chose you to be my husband/wife, and today I choose you again. Not because I should, not because it is expected, and not because I have no other choice, but because my love for you is even richer and deeper than the day I married you. I choose you again gladly and without reservation. Choosing each other is an ongoing process, my love, and every morning as I look at your wonderful face, I choose you anew and I rejoice that you have chosen me, too. How blessed I am to have you as my husband/wife. You have filled my life with joy, and I want to be married to you for the rest of my life, not because I should, or because it is expected, but because that is the longing of my heart.

Remember the first time we met? You were dancing with someone else. I cut in on that poor soul, and we have been dancing together ever since. Our life's dance has been a steady dance, weaving in and out of our days and years together. It's been a quiet, intimate dance of shared thoughts and dreams, through many summers of new-mown grass, and through cold, chilling winters. Today we continue our life's dance with a commitment that is as fresh and joyous as the day I married you. Dance with me, [husband or wife's name], for the rest of my life.

Reaffirmation ring vows

The following are vows that can be spoken during the ring exchange.

We have lived and loved as we promised long ago in the presence of God, and our past and our future are an unbroken circle, like this ring with which I renew my pledge to you of never ending devotion.

With this ring I reaffirm my love for you, a love refined in the crucible of our togetherness. Wear it as my prayer of thanksgiving and of my hopes for all our tomorrows.

First came the engagement ring, a promise of our wedding yet to come. Then came the gold band I placed on your finger on our wedding day, when I promised to love you and cherish you until the end of my days. Now comes this ring of renewal, celebrating our [number] precious years of married life together and the joyous years yet to come. With this ring I reaffirm my love for you.

Vow renewal wedding toasts

The following are toasts that can be used during the renewal celebration.

A toast for the husband or wife after their vow renewal ceremony

[Husband or wife's name], you're a very special man [or woman] and a very special husband [or wife]—loving, thoughtful and giving. You have the kind of strength that comes from your deep faith in God and the kind of wisdom that comes from knowing God's word. The life we have shared together for [number] years is a beautiful reflection of His love, and I thank God for you. Bless you, my dear husband [or wife].

A toast for the husband and wife, suitable for an older couple

I would like to propose a toast to [couple's names]. Sir Arthur Wing Pinero wrote these words: 'Those who love deeply never grow old; they may die of old age, but they die young.' May your love stay forever young.

A toast by the husband to his wife, suitable for an older couple

There is an old proverb that says: 'An old man in love is like a flower in winter.' [Wife's name], you have made me feel like a flower in winter. Thank you for marrying me [number] years ago today. To my bride.

A toast by the wife to her husband, suitable for an older couple

It has been said that there is no surprise as magical as finding your life's mate early in life. To love and be loved by you is like God's finger on my shoulder—an absolute miracle. To my dear husband.

A toast to the couple

I would like to propose a toast to [couple's names]. Our hearts were touched today as we witnessed the renewal of your wedding vows. You've been married for [number] years, and through those years, those of us who have known you, have been impressed by your constant love and support for each other. When you recited your wedding vows [number] years ago today, your love began to grow and carried you through good times and bad. Through sickness and health. Through times of plenty, and times when things weren't so great. But through it all, your love has overcome adversities, and your love has rejoiced in the good times as well. Here's to another [number] years of love and joy.

Life is better when it's shared by two. Your trials, triumphs, laughter, hopes, and tears all helped move you toward each other as you experienced them together. After [number] years of married life, you have become each other's dearest friend. Here's to another [number] years of sharing and loving.

Poignant touches for a vow renewal ceremony

Here are some touching elements to add to your vow renewal:

- Create exhibits and displays honoring the couple. Include their original wedding photos and marriage certificate, a photo of their first home, family photos, and sentimental memorabilia unique to the couple.

- The couple writes their own renewal vows.

- The couple's children each read a personalized tribute to their mom and dad and present them with a meaningful gift.

- The couple's grandchildren participate by performing a musical piece, reading an original poem, or presenting their grandparents with homemade wedding gifts.

- Friends and relatives offer poignant toasts, reflecting on what the couple has meant to them through the years.

- The couple's favorite song when they were dating is played for their first dance.

- The couple presents each other with newly designed wedding rings during the ring vows.

The renewal wedding honeymoon

You can't have a wedding ceremony without a honeymoon to follow. Plan something extra-special. Perhaps an exotic honeymoon destination, such as Hawaii, Fiji, or the Caribbean Islands. Or, how about a cruise? Maybe your dream is to return to your original honeymoon venue. That sounds especially romantic.

Chapter 7

Touching Ways to Personalize Your Wedding

It's a lovely idea to incorporate a few poignant additions to your ceremony. This will personalize your wedding and make it your very own one-of-a-kind wedding day. If you decide to incorporate one of the personal touches in this chapter into your ceremony, explain its meaning in your ceremony program. That way, your guests will be as touched as you are by the inclusion.

Handfasting Covenant Ceremony

This is an ancient Celtic marriage ceremony that has become popular since it was included in the movie *Braveheart*. The bride's right wrist is tied to the groom's left wrist during the ceremony. This is symbolic of the couple's commitment and devotion to each other. Many of today's ceremonies include handfasting as part of the marriage vows, regardless of the type of ceremony. Handfasting is sometimes called "hand tying" or "tying the knot." Once the bride's and groom's wrists are tied together, the deed is recognized as a binding contract between them and their lives become intertwined for all eternity. In fact, the act of handfasting becomes symbolic of the vows they have taken and their desire to become one.

Traditionally, a silk cord has been used. However, many variations of this ceremony have evolved, including the use of different materials and the way the tying takes place:

- In an African-American handfasting ceremony, the couple's hands may be tied together using a strip of Kente cloth, a length of braided grass, or a string of cowrie shells. The couple's hands may be tied by the officiant, a family member, or a close friend.

159

- During a Hindu wedding ceremony, a simple string is used to tie the couple's wrists together, a ritual known as *hasthagranthi*.

- During a Buddhist wedding ceremony, the fabric or rosary (known as the *mala*) is gently tied around the wrists of the bride and groom. The tying may be performed by the officiant or the couple's parents.

- A Christian couple may use the bride's prayer stole to tie their wrists together, as a symbol of their unity as a married couple and also of their united faith in God. After the officiant has tied their wrists together with the stole, he or she may also bless their union with the sign of the cross.

Wording for a handfasting covenant ceremony can be:

Officiant: *[Couple's names] have come here today to pledge their vows of marriage. [Groom's name], do you take [bride's name] to be your wife? Do you promise to love her, provide for her, and be faithful to her as long as you both shall live?*

Groom: *I do.*

Officiant: *[Bride's name], do you take [groom's name] to be your husband? Do you promise to love him, honor him, and be faithful to him as long as you both shall live?*

Bride: *I do.*

Officiant: *[Couple's name], present your wrists for the handfasting ceremony. As your wrists are fasted together by this cord (or cloth, plaid, string of cowrie shells, rope, string, braided grass, stole, etc.), you become bound to each other and to the vows you have promised.*

A toast for a handfasting ceremony can be:

We have witnessed your vows and your willingness to be bound together in marriage, symbolized by your poignant handfasting ceremony. We are all touched by your commitment and we, likewise, commit ourselves to you—to be there for you, to support you, and to encourage you as you venture out as a newly wedded couple. May you be filled with joy and unity throughout your married life. To [couple's names].

Commitment by Guests and Family Members

The officiant asks the guests and family members to stand as they witness the bride's and groom's wedding vows.

Following the couple's vows, the officiant turns to the congregation and asks: *Having witnessed [couple's names] recite their wedding vows, will each of you do everything in your power to uphold this couple in their marriage?*

Congregation: *We do.*

Incorporate Orange Blossoms

The bride wears orange blossoms in her hair. Orange blossoms have been symbolic of fertility and a happy marriage for centuries, going back to Greek and Spanish tradition. She may wear a cluster of orange blossoms, attached to the top of her veil or behind an ear, or she may wear a wreath of orange blossoms.

Bride and Groom Face the Guests

The bride and groom switch places with the officiant, which means they are facing their guests. This personalizes your wedding by getting your guests more closely involved in your ceremony.

Bride's Tribute to the Mothers

The bride carries two long-stemmed roses with her bouquet as she walks down the aisle. Before reaching the altar, she kisses her mother on her cheek as she presents her with one of the roses. Then, following the ceremony, the bride presents the second rose to her new mother-in-law, also with a kiss on the cheek. Another variation is for the bride to present the mothers with individual flowers pulled out of her bouquet. The bride may honor the grandmothers in the same way.

Designate an Honorary Attendant

An honorary attendant is someone very close to you who would have been a member of your wedding party if it were possible. For example, in the case of the groom's brother who's serving in the Army and can't come home for the wedding, he may be mentioned in the ceremony program with this suggested wording: *Honorary best man: Clinton Webster Jones, the groom's brother, currently serving in the U.S. Army*

Jumping the Broom

Jumping the broom is a meaningful African-American tradition, dating back to the 17th century. By jumping over the broom at the end of the ceremony, the bride and groom are symbolizing their love and commitment to each other as they establish a new beginning and a home of their own.

The traditional ritual is usually performed during the ceremony, after the officiant pronounces the couple husband and wife. It may also be performed in a glorious way during the wedding reception. The members of the wedding party precede the bride and groom into the reception venue. Then, just before the bride and groom enter, the broom is laid on the floor in front of them. They jump over the broom as they enter the reception hall, to the applause of their family and friends.

You can purchase a decorated broom, or you can decorate an everyday straw broom in your wedding colors with ribbons and flowers. You may also add small decorations in keeping with your wedding's theme. This broom will be displayed in the couple's home and cherished for all their married life.

Variations to the jumping the broom ceremony include:

- The guests may help decorate the broom prior to the ceremony or reception.
- During the ceremony or reception, the guests form a circle around the couple. The couple then uses their broom to sweep around the feet of the guests, a symbol of sweeping away the old and welcoming the new. Finally, the groom places the broom on the floor, holds his bride's hand and they jump over the broom, as the guests count: "One, two, three...jump!"
- The officiant may pronounce the couple husband and wife after they have jumped the broom, instead of before.

Something Old, Something New

The bride wears something old, something new, something borrowed, something blue, and a sixpence (or a penny) in her shoe. This ancient tradition is still honored today, although most brides haven't a clue where this came from or what it means.

Something old symbolizes continuity from generation to generation, such as Grandma's lace handkerchief, a piece of lace or ribbon from the bride's mother's or grandmother's wedding gown, or a piece of jewelry that has been handed down in the family. Something new symbolizes a glorious, happy future for the bride, such as her wedding gown. Something borrowed symbolizes joy and happiness, such as her sister's or best friend's pearl necklace or earrings. Something blue symbolizes fidelity and love, such as a blue lace garter, a blue ribbon sewn into the bride's petticoat or woven into her bridal bouquet. A sixpence or penny in her shoe assures the bride she'll be happy and lucky throughout her marriage.

Salted Bread and Grain

The bride sews salted bread into her petticoat and the groom carries grain in his pocket. This is an old German custom that assures future wealth and good luck.

Silk Cord Ceremony

The bride and groom are wrapped with a silk cord during the ceremony. This touching Mexican custom is symbolic of the joining of the bride and groom, to become one. The cord is wrapped over the couple's shoulders in a figure eight. Another option is for the couple to be joined with a lazo (a large set of double-looped rosary beads), symbolizing the binding of man and woman together in holy wedlock. In Mexico, the bride and groom kneel before the altar as they each hold a lighted candle and the priest wraps a single silver cord around their necks.

Care Cloth Ceremony

A care cloth is a rectangular piece of silk, linen, or tulle fabric, usually white with red trim. (A simple bridal veil may be purchased to serve as a care cloth. This is in addition to the veil the bride is wearing.) It may be draped over the head and shoulders of the bride and over the shoulders of the groom as they kneel at the altar, signifying a marriage yoke joining the bride and groom together. Another option is for the best man and maid or matron of honor to hold the care cloth over the heads of the kneeling couple. If the bride or groom has a child from a previous marriage, the child is often placed under the care cloth, between the bride and groom, symbolizing the acceptance of the child into the newly formed family.

Ceremony of the Loving Cup

The loving cup, or loving glass, is often used in Jewish and Christian wedding ceremonies. The bride and groom drink from the same cup, symbolizing the couple's becoming one on their wedding day. This cup is most often included in Jewish wedding ceremonies. The loving cup may be transported to the reception and used again by the bride and groom during the wedding feast. If the loving cup is used during the reception feast, it should be used before the meal begins, or after the meal is completed, before the dessert or cake cutting.

Variations of the loving cup include:

- The Scottish and Irish use a *quaich*, the Gaelic word for cup. This cup is a small silver or pewter bowl with two side handles. A double glass bottom provides a hiding place for a lock of the bride's hair.

- The French also use a double-handled goblet called a *coupe de marriage* (marriage cup). This goblet is quite ornate and eventually becomes a family heirloom. It is also a French tradition for the bride's godmother to present the bride with a loving cup before the wedding.

- German couples use a Nuremberg bridal beaker, made in southern Germany.

- American couples often use an existing family heirloom cup, or they have a new silver cup engraved with their names and wedding date.

It has become trendy to transport the loving cup from the ceremony to the reception to be used as a cake topper, instead of the traditional plastic bride and groom or wedding bells.

Blessing of the Coins

The blessing of the coins is also known as an *arrhae* ceremony. Coins are incorporated into wedding ceremonies as a symbol of earnest money or dower, the bride's portion of her husband's estate. The coins represent other things as well, such as the groom's promise to provide for his bride, and the blessing of God on the couple in a spiritual and financial way.

The giving, taking, and blessing of the coins are included in wedding ceremonies all over the world. Here are a few examples:

- France: The groom gives his bride thirteen coins, thirteen being considered a lucky number because it was the sum of Christ and His twelve apostles. The coins often have images stamped on them, such as two hands joined together, or inscriptions, such as "One Faith From Two Hearts." The coins are placed in a box and blessed during the service. The box is later placed in the couple's home to protect them and to remind them of financial responsibility.

- Philippines: The priest gives the groom a handful of coins, who then gives them to his bride. The bride then returns them to the priest. The process of pouring the coins from one hand to another symbolizes the grace of God being poured forth on the bride and groom.

- Scotland: The blessing of the coins is often included in a Scottish wedding ceremony. The coins may be antique coins used by the couple's parents or grandparents, or they may be new commemorative coins.

- Spain: The groom presents his bride with coins before the ceremony so she can carry them with her during the ceremony processional.

- Hungary: The groom gives his bride a bag of coins when she presents him with several handkerchiefs.

Wordings for coin blessings

The following are sample wordings for coin ceremonies:

Bless, O Lord, this earnest money, which today Thy servant [groom's name] puts into the hand of Thy handmaiden [bride's name], as Thou didst bless Abraham and Sarah, Isaac and Rebecca, Jacob and Rachel. Grant them the grace of Thy salvation, an abundance of things, and the constancy of work. May they flower as the rose planted in Jericho, and may they fear and adore our Lord Jesus Christ Thy Son, who liveth and reigneth with Thee, God the Father, in the unity of the Holy Spirit, God, forever and ever. Amen.

Bless, O Lord, these coins, which we bless in Thy name, entreating Thine immense clemency; that whoever is endowed with them may be divinely endowed with the riches of grace and glory—here, in eternity, and forever and ever. Amen.

O Lord God Almighty, who didst desire to bind Isaac with Rebecca in the likeness of holy matrimony through the transmission of Thy servant Abraham's earnest money so that a multitude of Children might spring forth by the offering of this gift; we beseech Thy might, that Thou, O Sanctifier, might approach the offering of this earnest money which Thy servant [groom's name] giveth to his beloved spouse [bride's name], and that Thou mayest kindly bless them along with their gifts. May they rejoice happily together as they are blessed by Thy protection and joined by the bond of love, and may they be forever delivered with Thy faithful ones. Through our Lord Jesus Christ Thy Son, who liveth and reigneth with Thee in the unity of the Holy Spirit, God, forever and ever. Amen.

Groom (to his bride): *Receive these coins, they are a pledge of the care I will take so that we will not lack what is necessary in our home.*

Bride (to her groom): *I receive them as a sign of the care I will take so that our home will prosper.*

Giving of the coins during the ring vows

The coins, or "earnest money," may be given as part of the ring exchange. Today's couple's often use sentimental coins from places that have special meaning to them, such as a subway token from the city where they met, or coins saved from their visits to foreign countries. Here are a couple wordings:

[Bride's name], with this ring I thee wed, with this silver I thee endow, and with my body I thee honor. In honor of God and of holy Lady Mary and of all the saints and of my lord.

With this ring I thee wed, with my body I thee honor, and with this dower (the coins) I thee endow.

Lighting of the Unity Candle

This tradition has become popular in the last 15 years or so because of its rich meaning. After the bride and groom have recited their vows, they walk together to the unity candle, which is a large candle that sits unlighted between two smaller lighted candles that represent the two families. The bride and groom each lift a smaller candle and, together, light the larger unity candle, symbolizing their marriage to each other and that two families have become one.

A variation of this ceremony is for the parents of the bride and groom, or the couple's children, to participate. The bride's parents and/or children help hold the bride's candle as the flame is used to light the unity candle. The groom's parents and/or children do the same.

Ceremony of the Rose Covenant

A rose covenant ceremony adds meaning to any wedding. It can take place at any venue, indoors or outdoors, but it's especially poignant for an outdoor garden ceremony. This ceremony usually follows the recitation of the couple's formal wedding vows, and is introduced by the officiant:

Officiant: *[Couple's names] will now participate in the ceremony of the rose. [Groom's name] holds a long-stemmed rose that he will present to [bride's name] as she holds a vase filled with water. The water in the vase symbolizes the protection and nourishment their marriage with provide to each other.*

Groom (as he hands his bride a long-stemmed white rose): *[Bride's name], take this rose as a symbol of my love. It began as a tiny bud and blossomed, just as my love has grown and blossomed for you.*

Bride (as she places the rose into a bud vase, filled with water): *I accept this rose, a symbol of your love, and I place it into water, a symbol of life. For, just as this rose cannot survive without water, I cannot survive without you.*

Groom: *In remembrance of this day, I will give you a white rose each year on our anniversary, as a reaffirmation of my love and the vows spoken here today.*

Bride: *And I will refill this vase with water each year, ready to receive your gift, in reaffirmation of the new life you have given me and the vows spoken here today.*

Groom (as he and his bride join hands around the vase): *And so, this rose will be a symbolic memory of my commitment to you this hour; I vow to be a faithful husband to you, to comfort you, honor you, respect you, and cherish you all the days of my life.*

Bride (as they continue to hold the vase together): *And I commit myself to you, to be a faithful wife, to comfort you, honor you, respect you, and cherish you all the days of my life.*

Variations of the rose ceremony include:

- Following the rose ceremony, the couple's families also exchange roses during a musical interlude.

- Following the rose ceremony, the bride presents a rose to her mother and the groom presents one to his mother.

- If the bride or groom has children from a previous marriage, each may present a rose to the other's child. For example, the bride may present a rose to her groom's son, and the groom may present a rose to his bride's daughter.

Ceremony of the Blessing Stones

A blessing stones ceremony, also known as a wishing stones ceremony, may be incorporated into any type of wedding ceremony. There are many variations of this ceremony, but each has the same purpose, casting a good wish or a blessing upon the couple during or after the ceremony.

Stones and note cards are given to the guests as they arrive at the ceremony site. The purpose of the blessing stones ceremony is explained to the guests.

The stones may be gleaming, polished agates, or any attractive stones. Or, if the wedding is being held outdoors, in a forested area, by a lake or a river, the guests may be asked to gather their own stones from the site, before the ceremony begins.

Once each guest has a stone in hand, whether it was given to him or he gathered it from the site, he is asked to write a personalized wedding blessing or wish for the couple on the card. The cards may be preprinted with "helper introductions," such as "My wish for Jim and Sandy is that..." or "May Jim and Sandy be blessed with...."

During the ceremony, the officiant explains the meaning of the blessing stones, and the personal wishes or blessing each guest is asked to describe on the note cards.

The guests may be asked to read their blessings or wishes for the couple as part of the ceremony or during the wedding reception to follow. In either case, as the guests read off their note cards, they toss their stones into a water-filled container that has been provided for this purpose. They place their note cards in a decorative basket.

The water-filled container becomes a cherished possession the newly-weds display in a prominent place in their home for years to come.

Variations of the blessing stones ceremony include:

- If the ceremony takes place outdoors next to a body of water, each guest is asked to throw his or her stone into the water, as each recites his or her blessing or wish for the couple.

- If the ceremony takes place on an ocean beach, instead of stones, each guest is asked to find a beautiful seashell. The shells are then placed in a container as each guest recites a blessing or a wish.

Covenant of Salt or Sand

This covenant ceremony can be performed using salt or sand. If the wedding takes place on a sandy beach, it's especially meaningful to perform this ceremony using sand. Whether salt or sand is used for this ceremony, however, the meaning is the same.

The bride and groom each hold a bag or glass container of salt or sand (the salt or sand may be the same color or different colors). These containers of salt or sand represent their individual lives, with all they were, all they are, and all they will ever be. The bride and groom willingly empty their containers of salt or sand into a larger container, symbolizing the joining of their lives for eternity. Just as the grains of sand can never be separated and returned to their individual containers, so the couple is now no longer two, but one, never to be separated one from the other.

During this ceremony, the officiant may say the following:

This covenant relationship is symbolized through the pouring of these two individual bags of salt—one representing you, [bride's name], and all that you were, all that you are, and all that you will ever be, and the other representing you, [groom's name], and all that you were and all that you are, and all that you will ever be. As these two bags of salt are poured into the third bag, the individual bags of salt will no longer exist, but will be joined together as one. Just as these grains of salt can never be separated and poured again into the individual bags, so will your marriage be. Far more important than your individuality is now the reality that you are no longer two, but one, never to be separated one from the other.

The bride and groom empty their individual bags of salt into a third bag.

[Couple's names], we have heard your vows and you've symbolized your union by pledging your lives to each other, exchanging rings, and through the covenant of salt [or sand]. So, by the authority of God's word and the state of [state's name], as a minister of the Gospel, I now pronounce you husband and wife.

Instead of using salt or sand, water may be used. The bride and groom each hold a container of clear or colored water which are poured into one container, signifying a union of two lives that can never be separate again. Another idea is to use "sentimental" sand for this ceremony. For example, the bride's sand may come from a beach where she played as a child, or the groom's may be from the beach where he asked his bride to marry him.

Memorial Tribute

Memorial tributes are popular at today's wedding ceremonies. The bride may display a small floral wreath on a stand beside the altar as a tribute to her father who recently passed away, or the groom may include a written tribute to his grandfather in the ceremony program. The couple may light a memorial candle in honor of a loved one, or the bride and groom may carry or wear a memento that belonged to the loved one.

An appropriate memorial toast to a loved one may sound like this:

Please raise your glasses in a memorial toast to [Judy's grandma, Jim's Uncle Howard, and so on]. We know he/she would have loved to be here to see (daughter, grandson, etc.) be married to [bride or groom's name]. But we know he/she is here in spirit. Wouldn't he/she have loved to see [bride's name] walk down the aisle— what a beautiful bride! We miss him/her and we toast him/her now in memory of his/her life and positive influence on all our lives. To [loved one's name].

Honor Your Parents and Grandparents at Your Reception

Gather wedding photos and wedding day memorabilia from your parents and grandparents to create a display at your wedding reception. You may be able to resurrect Grandma's gown or veil, or maybe the gloves she wore at her wedding. Dig deep and see what you can find. Not only will this be an interesting display, but it will be honoring, as well.

Renewal of Marriage Vows by the Guests

Following the couple's marriage vows, the officiant asks all married couples to stand and renew their marriage vows. The officiant prompts the husbands and wives, as they hold hands and look into each others' eyes and renew their vows. This is especially touching for a Valentine's Day or New Year's wedding, when the guests are already in a mushy, romantic mood.

Ring the Church Bells

The bride and groom ring the church's bell together after the ceremony. This is a lovely tradition, letting everyone in the community know that the ceremony is over and that the couple is overjoyed. The couple may climb up into a tower to ring the bells by hand, or, if the bells are electronically controlled, the church's custodial staff may ring the bells on cue from the bride and groom.

Dove Release

If you're planning a daytime wedding, you may want to consider a dove display and release. White love doves have always been symbols of holiness, love, and fidelity. They may be displayed in a gilded cage on the guest book table before your ceremony, and on your head table during your wedding reception.

The doves may be released as the bride and groom ring the church bells, or as a uniquely special activity. Alternatively, they may be released as you run to your getaway vehicle after the reception. The important factor is that the doves must be released during the day with enough hours of daylight left for them to fly back to their permanent homes.

Include Your Favorite Readings in Your Ceremony

You may have a favorite portion of classical literature, verses of Scripture, song lyrics, poetry, or a personal love letter from your fiancée. Readings are entirely optional, but if you decide to include one in your ceremony, it may be placed anywhere you like in the order of service. Also, as another way to give meaning to your wedding, ask dear friends or family members to participate, each reading one selection. You may also ask a child to read something that's meaningful to you and your fiancée. Your readings may be printed within your ceremony programs, or they may be copied onto parchment paper, which can be rolled into scrolls, tied with ribbons, and given to your guests as mementos of your wedding.

What the Groom Needs to Know

Write a surprise love letter to your bride to be read by someone during the wedding ceremony. You can tell her how lucky you were to meet her that day (at the supermarket, the ball game, on campus) and how she has filled a void in your life, and so on. Your love letter will stand head and shoulders above any other readings that could possibly be included in your ceremony.

Life Renewal Ceremony

A life renewal ceremony, also known as a new life ceremony, is for couples where one or both are recovering from addictions, such as to alcohol or drugs. It's an especially meaningful ceremony because, not only is the ceremony a celebration of the couple's love for each other, but also a celebration of their recovery.

This renewal ceremony is especially poignant for the guests and family members, who vow to love, encourage, and support the couple through all the years of their married life together. Candle lighting is incorporated into this ceremony as well, where all the guests hold their lighted candles high as they pledge their vow of commitment. If the wedding is small and intimate, the friends and family members form a circle around the couple as they witness their vows, and pledge their commitment of support to the couple.

Following is an example of a life renewal ceremony, personalized for the couple:

Convocation

Officiant: *We have gathered here today to witness the marriage of [couple's names]. However, not only do we rejoice with them as they marry and embark on their life together as husband and wife, we also share their joy as they experience together the victory of new life through recovery and renewal. The victory they share is a gift they will treasure throughout all the years of their married life, a treasured gift for which they will give thanks, with tears of laughter and joy.*

Invocation

Officiant: *Thank you for bringing [couple's names] together. Thank you for the love you have given them toward each other. May your love encircle them during this service, and may their marriage be richly filled with the love and joy only You can bring. Amen.*

Reading

The bride's cousin reads the following from Ecclesiastes 4, verses 9 through 12: *Two are better than one, because they have a good reward for their toil. For if they fall, one will lift up his fellow; but woe to him who is alone when he falls and has not another to lift him up. Again, if two lie together, they are warm; but how can one be warm alone? And though a man might prevail against one who is alone, two will withstand him.*

Expression of intent

Officiant (to the bride): *[Bride's name], is it your intent to marry [groom's name] today? To bond to him as his wife?*

Bride: *Yes.*

Officiant (to the groom): *[Groom's name], is it your intent to marry [bride's name] today? To bond to her as her husband?*

Groom: *Yes.*

Vows

Groom (to his bride): *[Bride's name], you are my healer, my comforter, and the joy of my life. Your love has restored my torn, broken heart; your smile has healed my pain; and your caring spirit has rescued mine from the dark places. May our love be always bright, always beautiful and always new. [Bride's name], I vow to be a faithful, loving husband, to care for you, to comfort you and to cherish you for as long as we both shall live.*

Bride (to her groom): *[Groom's name], you are the sunshine of my life after the storms, my sweet nectar after the painful seasons of my days. I am proud to marry you this day and become your wife. Our lives have been touched by a very special love, as soft as the dawn, as radiant as the sun, and as beautiful as a rainbow that enfolds us after a storm. [Groom's name], I promise to be faithful to you, to honor you, to suffer with you, and to rejoice with you for as long as we both shall live.*

Ring exchange

Officiant: *Now, may I have a token of your sincerity that you will keep these vows?*

The best man gives the bride's ring to the officiant who holds it up and says: *This ring is a symbol of your vows and wearing it bears witness to your marital fidelity.*

The officiant hands the bride's ring to the groom and instructs him to place it on her finger.

Officiant (to the groom): *Do you, [groom's name], give this ring to [bride's name] as a token of your love and fidelity, and as a sign of the bond of new life and renewal?*

Groom: *I do.*

The officiant takes the groom's ring from the maid or matron of honor and gives it to the bride, instructing her to place it on her groom's finger.

Officant (to the bride): *Do you, [bride's name], give this ring to [groom's name] as a token of your love and fidelity, and as a sign of the bond of new life and renewal?*

Bride: *"I do."*

Communal candlelight vows

Officiant (addressing the guests, who were each given un-lighted candles as they entered the ceremony venue): *You have just witnessed the marriage vows of [couple's names]. Please rise as you participate in the communal candlelight vows of support for this couple, pledging to love them, encourage them, and support them through all their years of married life.*

Officiant (addressing the bride and groom, as he lights a candle for each of them): *[Couple's names], please use your lighted candles to light the candles of your family and friends.*

The bride and groom light the candles of the first guest sitting on their respective sides of the ceremony venue. These guests then turn to the next person, lights his or her candle, and so on, until everyone in the venue holds a lighted candle.

Officiant (addressing the guests): *Please raise your candles high and repeat these vows after me: "We vow to support [couple's names]. We will love them and encourage them throughout all the years of their lives."*

The officiant thanks the guests and asks them to extinguish their candles.

Pronouncement of marriage

Officiant: *And now, by the power vested in me by the laws of the state of [state name], I pronounce you husband and wife. You may kiss your bride.*

Benediction

Officiant: *Bless this couple as they go forth into their life together as husband and wife. May they each give thanks to their higher power who has answered their prayers and given the gifts of love, renewal and new life. God grant them the serenity to accept the things they cannot change, the courage to change the things they can, and the wisdom to know the difference. Amen.*

A wedding toast to the bride and groom, suitable for a life renewal wedding reception

I would like to propose a toast to [couple's names]. Today is a special day for both of you—a day of new life and beginnings. A day of hope for a future filled with sweet joy and peace. We're so glad you found each other. Will everyone please raise their glasses and join me in a heartfelt toast to [couple's names].

[Couple's names], I can speak for everyone in this room when I say that we're overjoyed you found each other. You found healing balm in each other's love and compassion. To your future—a life filled with peace and laughter.

Dad's Giving-Away Words

Here's a new trend: When the pastor asks the bride's father, "Who gives this woman to be married to this man?" Instead of simply saying, "Her mother and I do," the bride's dad gives a little speech about his daughter before he gives her away to the groom.

A famous example can be found on *www.godvine.com*. The is video is entitled "Father of the bride gives the most touching speech ever"; it's a touching example of giving-away words.

Here are other examples of giving-away speechs:

Officiant: *Who gives this woman to be married to this man?*

Bride's Father: *Her Mom and I do, but first I'd like to tell a little story. Twenty-three years ago, [bride's name] was born at Memorial Hospital. I remember it as if it were yesterday. I wore a groove into the hallway outside the delivery room as I paced away. And when the nurse laid you in my arms, I cried—you were an incredibly beautiful baby. But that was just the beginning. You have been a joy to Mom and me ever since. We are so proud of your accomplishments. I remember your first piano recital, your winning basket at the state's basketball championship, and your recent graduation with honors from USC. And weren't you a lucky girl to choose that school, because that's where you met this guy. (Looks at the groom with a smile.) I can't imagine what you saw in him—just because he happens to be a handsome attorney with a bright future, and just because he happens to adore you. I've only known you for about a year [groom's name], but I've got to say that Mom and I are overjoyed with her choice. I'm proud and happy for both of you. Mom and I give you (the bride) to this man without reservation. God bless you both.*

||||||||||||||||||||||||||||||||||||||||||||||||||||||||||||||||||||||||

I'd like to say a few words. [Bride's name], you know you're 'Daddy's Little Girl.' You always have been and you always will be. But it's time for you to leave our home and live forever with [groom's name]. You and [groom's name] will start a family of your own, and I'll be a grandpa to your little ones. But even then, you'll still be my little girl. It's hard to let you go—I'm sure you know that—we've always been so close. But, as Mom and I have gotten to know this guy (glances at the groom), we know you've made the perfect choice. You are so right for each other, and it is with our blessings that Mom and I give you to him today.

||||||||||||||||||||||||||||||||||||||||||||||||||||||||||||||||||||||||

[Bride's name], do you remember when you were little and I used to read you a bedtime story every night? You always loved the fairy tales about princesses and knights in shining armor. Well, honey, today you're a beautiful princess yourself, and you're marrying your knight in shining armor. Mom and I are overjoyed for both of you as we give you to [groom's name].

Include Ethnic Dances
During the Wedding Reception

Choose your family's favorites, such as:

- The Horah (Israeli folk dance).
- Cielito Lindo (Mexican).
- The Highland Fling (Scottish).
- The Irish Jig (Irish folk dance).
- The Tarantella (Italian).
- The Handkerchief Dance (Greek folk dance).
- The Dollar Dance (European tradition where money is pinned on the bride's gown or the groom's jacket, in payment for the privilege of dancing with him or her).
- The music your parents chose for their first dances at their wedding receptions (ask your reception host, the DJ, or the bandleader to make a special announcement introducing the music).

Include Your Family's
Ethnic Dishes at the Reception

If you plan to hire a catering service, don't engage their services until you find out whether they will agree to use your family's recipes for the reception meal. If you're furnishing all the reception food yourself, ask various family members to make family favorites for the reception. If this will require great expense, the family members may offer to create these special dishes in lieu of wedding gifts.

Embrace your ethnic heritage by serving a traditional nuptial bread. Many countries and cultures have one of these breads in their wedding traditions, such as:

- Crete: A special braided bread.
- Poland: Rye bread with salt.
- Norway: *Brudlaupskling*, a beautiful Norwegian bread.
- Ukraine: *Korovai*, an elaborately decorated bread.

- Russia: A ritual takes place where bread and salt are tasted together during the wedding feast.

- Greece: Sourdough wedding breads are served that have been decorated with beads and flower blossoms.

- Caribbean: A fruitcake soaked in rum.

- England: A wedding fruitcake with a top tier called the "christening cake," which is saved for the baptism of the couple's first child.

- Scotland and Ireland: An oatcake is ritually broken over the head of the bride as she crosses the threshold of her new home, after bourbon-laced fruitcake was served during the reception.

Similarly, there are ethnic wedding cakes:

- Greece: The wedding cake is baked with these added ingredients: honey, sesame seeds, and quince.

- Japan: The showy wedding cake on display during the reception is actually an enormous Styrofoam dummy cake that includes elaborate decorations. The guests are served "real" cake on plates from the kitchen.

- Holland: The wedding cake is decorated with pink or white marzipan roses.

- Denmark: Called a *kransekage*, a Danish wedding cake is composed of 18 layers of almond-meringue rings.

- France: The wedding cake may consist of stacked sponge cakes decorated with confectioner's cream, flavored with fruit liqueur. An alternative is the *croquembouche*, a pyramid-style wedding cake consisting of decorated cream puffs, covered with carmelized sugar.

- Jamaica: The wedding cake is a dark cake which includes raisins, dried fruits, and fruit peels that have been soaked in rum for two weeks before the cake is baked.

- Bermuda: Instead of a traditional cake top, the cake-topper is a small sapling, which symbolizes the couple's new life together.

Include an Ethnic Toast
During Your Reception

The following are words of well wishes in different languages and from different cultures:

- Albanian: *Nga mot gezuar*! (Happiness for many years.)

- Angolan: *A sua felicidade!* (To your happiness!)

- Arabic: *Besehtak!* (To your health!)

- Argentinean: *Salud!* (To your health!)

- Austrian: *Prosit!* (May it be to your health!)

- British: All good things to you! May your journey be good, on the road that you choose, though it be fast or slow, and joy attend you all the way whichever road you go. (An old Yorkshire toast.)

- German: *Ein Prosit der Gemutlichkeit!* (A toast to easygoing, happy-go-lucky living!)

- Greek: *Stin ygia sou!* (To your health!)

- Haitian: *A votre santé!* (To your health!)

- Hawaiian: *Kou ola kino!* (To your health!)

- Native American: Now, as you join your life together, intertwining your pasts, weaving them into one future, may the texture be especially strong, and may your pattern be especially beautiful.

- Irish: Here's to health, peace, and prosperity; May the flower of love never be nipped by the frost of disappointment. May there always be work for your hands to do. May your purse always hold a coin or two. May the sun always shine on your windowpane. May a rainbow be certain to follow each rain. May the hand of a friend always be near you. May God fill your hearts with gladness to cheer you.

- Italian: *Viva l'amor!* (Long live love!)

- Japanese: *Konotabi wa omedeto gozaimasu!* (Congratulations to the bride and groom!)

- Jewish: *L'chayim!* (To life! To your health!)

- Korean: *Chu-kha-ham-ni-da!* (Congratulations!)
- Mexican: *Salud y tu amor!* (To your health, and to your love!)
- Polish: *Na zdrowie, azeby nasze dzieci mialy bogatych rodzicow!* (To our health! May our children have rich parents!)
- Portuguese: *Saude e gozo!* (Health and enjoyment!)
- Romanian: *Noroc!* (Good luck!)
- Russian: *Za Zdorovie molodech!* (To the health of the young couple!)
- Thai: *Chai yo!* (To your health and well-being!)
- Turkish: *Serefinize!* (To your honor.)
- Venezuelan: *A la salud!* (To your health!)
- Welsh: *Eichid da, a whye fahr!* (Good health and lots of fun!)

Include Other Ethnic Traditions in Your Wedding

Here are samples of wedding traditions from different cultures:

- China: The bride and groom drink together from goblets of honey and wine that have been tied together with red ribbon. To the Chinese, the color red symbolizes courage and joy. Thus, when the couple shares the wedding cup by drinking from the goblets at the same time, this symbolizes the bride and groom coming together in the joy of love, and the courage it will require. Another Chinese wedding custom is for the guests to set off fire-crackers after the ceremony. This is to scare away evil spirits.

- Egypt: The bride's right wrist is tied to the groom's left wrist during the ceremony or the reception.

- Croatia: After the ceremony, the bride and groom circle a well three times as they toss apples into the well, symbolizing a fruitful marriage.

- Denmark: At the end of the wedding reception, the groom's family members encircle the groom and cut his tie and socks, symbolizing the undressing of the groom before the wedding night. The pieces of tie and socks are then auctioned off to raise money for the couple's honeymoon.

- Finland: During the wedding reception, a plate is balanced on the bride's head during the couple's first dance. When it falls to the floor and breaks, the pieces are counted, symbolizing the number of children the couple will have. Also, a waltz is always the last dance of the reception during which the bride and groom are kept apart; the women dance with the bride, and the men with the groom. Finally, at the end of the waltz the bride and groom are allowed to dance with each other.

- Israel: The bride and groom both wear white during the wedding ceremony, symbolizing a state of purity as they become husband and wife.

- Japan: During the wedding reception, the bride and groom both drink a toast from a two-handled cup, a symbol of life. Drinking the toast together symbolizes the joining of two lives. This cup is cherished and handed down through the family for years to come.

- Greece: The bride and groom each carry a candle decorated with ribbons and flowers. The candles symbolize their love for each other and their delight to marry each other. The candles also symbolize the illumination they intend to bring into each other's lives. Also, a Greek bride may tuck a lump of sugar inside her glove, symbolizing a sweet marriage.

- Germany: Traditionally, the groom gives the bride a pair of elaborately decorated slippers. This is said to demonstrate that he will be the head of the family. However, another tradition says that a wife who assumes this role is said to "have her husband under her slipper."

- Philippines: During the wedding reception, the bride and groom eat their wedding feast off one shared plate. Also, a money dance is part of the festivities where guests pin money on the bride's and groom's clothes. Their families consider the money dance to be a competition to see which will receive the most money.

- The Netherlands: The bride and groom sit on chairs or thrones, under a canopy of boughs of fresh evergreens. This is where they receive the well wishes of their friends, family, and guests during the wedding rehearsal or wedding reception. The fresh evergreen boughs symbolize the freshness and vitality of their love and commitment to each other.

- India: In this country, the pleasant fragrance of flowers has deep spiritual significance. At a wedding, spilled flower petals speak to this blessing: "May your life together be filled with comfort, ease, and the fragrance of flowers." This is why the groom's brother drops flower petals onto the bride and groom at the end of the marriage ceremony. Another tradition is for the bride and groom to exchange floral garlands, during which time they are tied together with a sash as they walk around a ceremonial fire seven times. This symbolizes their vow to face life's problems together as man and wife.

- Indonesia: A wedding tradition is followed whereby the bride and groom are ushered into a quiet room before the ceremony. This is to protect them from anxious friends and family members and any evil spirits who may wish to harm them. This quiet time alone is a calming time for the couple right before the wedding.

- Bermuda: The bride and groom traditionally plant a tree in their garden, symbolizing new life and continuing life. As the tree grows, so does the deep commitment of the couple's love for each other.

- Islamic countries: A henna ritual is often performed before the wedding by artists who specialize in intricate henna designs. These henna designs decorate the hands and feet of the bride. Occasionally, the groom's hands and feet are also decorated in this way.

- African-American: Many African-American couples include a Kwanzaa ceremony during their wedding. Although this ceremony usually takes place during a December wedding, it may be included any month of the year. The officiant charges the bride and groom to practice the seven principles of Kwanzaa. The couple accepts this charge by lighting seven candles as they state their intention to follow the principles of unity, self-determination, collective work and responsibility, collective economics, purpose, creativity, and faith.

- England, Bulgaria, Scotland, and Italy: When the wedding ceremony takes place in a small village, it is a custom for the bride, her wedding party, and her guests to walk to church. A flower girl tosses flower petals and sprigs of ivy along the path ahead of them. The flower petals denote a smooth, happy married life. The ivy denotes fidelity. The bride hopes to see a chimney sweep along the way, a symbol of good luck. To assure good luck, some brides even invite chimney sweeps to their weddings. A horseshoe is also considered good luck, so a bride often carries a decorated horseshoe, streaming with ribbons, as she walks to the church. This horseshoe is later hung over the door of the couple's home.

- England: Someone places a live or fake spider on the bride's gown, which is said to bring good luck to the bride on her wedding day.

- France: It is traditional for the wedding guests to bring fresh flowers with them to the ceremony which are used to decorate the wedding venue.

- Indonesia: The wedding ceremony takes place in front of a statue that spouts water. The symbolism of the flowing water is the overflowing love between the couple and their families. Another tradition is for the bride's mother to place a floral garland around the groom's neck, showing him that he has been accepted by the bride's family.

- Italy: The couple's family members place an enormous ribbon at the church's entranceway, symbolizing the spiritual tie that will bind the bride and groom.

- Korea: Ducks are often included in the processional, symbolizing wedding fidelity, because ducks mate for life.

- Scotland: Immediately after the bride and groom exchange their wedding vows, the groom drapes a shawl of his clan's tartan over the bride's shoulders. This symbolizes the acceptance of the bride into the groom's clan.

- Switzerland: During the wedding processional, junior bridesmaids toss brightly colored handkerchiefs to the wedding guests.

Each guest who catches one is expected to contribute money to the newlyweds.

- Polynesia: The bride and groom hold hands during the entire wedding ceremony, and after the wedding kiss, they touch noses as a sign of affection.

- Czech Republic: Rosemary is a symbol of fertility and is worn by the bride and her bridesmaids. The bride's mother usually weaves rosemary into a bridal wreath, or crown, which the bride wears during the ceremony.

- Sweden: The bride places a gold coin, a gift from her mother, in her right shoe. She places a silver coin, a gift from her father, in her left shoe. These coins assure the bride that she will always be well cared for. Also, the bride wears her bridal shoes unfastened, symbolizing an easy childbirth.

- Puerto Rico: A doll is placed in the center of the bride's and groom's table during the wedding reception.

Give Your Guests Crystal or Brass Bells

During the reception, present each of your guests with a crystal or brass bell. The bell serves three purposes: they can ring their bells as they send you off after the wedding reception, the bells serve as wedding favors, and the bells can serve as Christmas tree ornaments, to remind the guests of your wedding day.

Make a Wedding Time Capsule

Use a box or other container as your "capsule," and fill it with memorabilia from your wedding day: your wedding invitation, ceremony program, copy of the best man's toast, reception menu, wedding photos, a CD containing your vows and/or wedding music, a DVD of your ceremony, pieces of ribbon from your bridal bouquet, a bottle of your favorite wine, and (this is the best part) love letters written to each other on your wedding day. Store the capsule away in a safe place and open it on your 10th wedding anniversary.

Include a Wedding Quilt at Your Reception

Perhaps an aunt or your grandmother will make you a wedding quilt. If not, purchase one and have it available during the reception for your guests and family members to sign with a permanent fabric marking pen on the plain side of the quilt.

Another option is to ask your guests to sign a tablecloth with a fabric pen. Their signatures can be embroidered later on. Use this tablecloth on your wedding anniversaries.

Include a Group Candle Lighting Ceremony

Present the guests with decorated candles as they arrive for the ceremony. Then, preceding the officiant's final wedding blessing, have an usher or groomsman light the candles of the guests seated on the inside aisles of the venue. The guests then light the candle of the next guest, and so on, until all the guests have lighted candles. The officiant then asks everyone to raise their candles high, symbolizing their participation in the final wedding blessing. For the best dramatic effect, include this ceremony at the end of an evening wedding.

Include Your Pet in Your Wedding

It's become trendy to include a pet in a wedding. In fact, even Carrie Underwood, Tori Spelling, Gwen Stefani, and Adam Sandler included their pets in their ceremonies. Adam's dog served as his best man and wore a tux and a yarmulke on its head.

If this idea appeals to you, consider your pet's personality and temperament. Do you really think it's a good idea? If so, the first step is to find out whether pets are allowed at your ceremony and/or reception venues. If you are planning a formal religious ceremony, such as Catholic rites in a cathedral, for example, it's unlikely that a pet will be allowed, unless you obtain the permission of the priest.

Here are ways your pet can participate:

- The bride may hold her pet in her arms as she walks down the aisle, or she may hold her cat in her arms during the wedding vows. One bride really wowed the guests when she was accompanied down the aisle by her adorable pot-bellied pig, all dressed up in wedding finery.
- Be your maid of honor or best man.
- Be your flower girl by carrying a basket of flowers in its teeth, or by pulling a petal cart that drops flower petals along the aisle as

the dog pulls the cart. (Petal carts are available at pet boutiques and online.)

- During the processional, the groom may walk down the aisle next to his bride with his dog on a leash.

- Be your ring bearer by wearing a ring bearer pillow collar or by tying a satin bag to its collar. You may pretend to forget who has the rings, then have Duke bring them down the aisle attached to his collar. One couple trained their pet owl to fly down the aisle with the rings tied to its legs.

- Be led down the aisle by the bride, one of the bridesmaids, or, in the case of a small pet, a child or teenager. For example, a flower girl or ring bearer may be able to lead the pet down the aisle as they perform their "regular" duties, or they may pull the pet inside a decorated wagon.

- Your cat may be placed inside a beautifully decorated cage next to the groomsmen or bridesmaids. A caged pet may also be set on the table next to the guest book prior to the ceremony.

- A bird may be placed in a cage, set on a perch, or in the case of a parrot or cockatoo, be taught to speak during the wedding. One couple trained their parrot to say, "You may kiss the bride." A really smart bird may be trained to fly from the rear of the venue to deliver the ring(s). One bride walked down the aisle with her pet parrot on her arm.

- A pet horse provides a treasured photo opp. You probably won't bring it into the ceremony venue, but the bride or groom can pose atop its back after the reception.

- If your wedding or ceremony venue won't allow pets, use your pet as a "greeter" outside the door of the venue as the guests enter.

The most common pet included in a wedding ceremony is a dog, which will require that you hire a dog handler for the day, preferably someone your pet is already comfortable with, but not someone who'll be a member of your wedding party. A handler can keep your animal from becoming overwhelmed by taking it on a calm neighborhood walk and giving it water and potty breaks. Some handlers even prefer to bring the dog's cage, bed, blanket, treats, and toys from home. This gives the dog a cozy, familiar place to relax and maybe even take a little nap. It also provides an opportunity for the dog handler to take a break. If your dog decides to bark or act out during the ceremony, the handler can discretely remove it from the venue. I know of one case where the groom had a "Best Dog" instead of a best man. The dog was perfectly calm and well-behaved until a soprano began to sing during the ceremony. This triggered something in the dog to make it howl, which was funny, of course, but did require a quick exit from the building

If your ceremony or reception will take place outdoors, that solves a lot of problems, especially when it comes to dogs. You'll still need a handler or pet sitter to watch over your pet and see that any messes are cleaned up immediately.

When it comes to wedding attire for your pet, you'll find hundreds of choices online, everything from doggie wedding gowns and tuxes, to bridesmaid dresses, to ring bearer collar pillows, to exquisite wedding collars and leads.

In Chapter 2, you read about wedding day insurance, which I highly recommend, especially if you plan to include your pet in your ceremony or reception. Also, your ceremony or reception venue may charge you a fee to include your pet. This fee is to cover any extra cleaning that needs to be done due to a pet potty accident or lingering pet hair. If you do decide to include your pet in your wedding day, you'll be glad you did. Several couples I've talked with say they cherish the wedding photos that included their pets, especially after the pets passed away.

Practice with your pet ahead of time, whether walking down the aisle, pulling a petal cart, wearing a floral wreath, wearing the wedding attire, or being around crowds of people. If you plan to hire a pet handler or pet sitter, have that person work with your pet in the months preceding the wedding. Also, be sure your handler is present at the wedding rehearsal to go through the motions with your pet. By the way, if things don't go well with your pet at the rehearsal, be flexible and reconsider the idea of including your pet after all.

‖‖

Etiquette 101

Here are some things to remember when including a pet in your wedding:

- No puppies or kittens.
- No "biters"—if your dog bites, leave him at home.
- No food or water within two hours of the ceremony.
- No food or water for the pet during the ceremony.
- Hire or appoint a pet handler to be in full charge of your pet.
- Bathe and groom your pet beforehand, to prevent pet odors or allergic reactions from guests.
- If your pet has allergies, play it safe and assemble the pet's floral wreath, if planned, out of artificial flowers.

‖‖

Part 3

The Wedding Reception

This section is all about formal and informal receptions. A formal reception, as with a formal ceremony, comes with rules of etiquette regarding such things as:

- Choice of venue.
- Order of the receiving line.
- Reception theme.
- Site and table decor.
- Table settings.
- Use of place cards.
- Type of food service.
- The music.
- Dance order.
- Wedding toasts.
- How to display wedding gifts.
- The couple's get-away.

An informal reception, as with an informal ceremony, is less restrictive in every way:

- It may be held anywhere you like, such as your church's social hall, on a ferry boat, or at the beach.
- You can include your pet at your reception. In fact, Chapter 9 contains a special "wedding toast" from the bride's dog.
- The food service can be anything from a light brunch buffet to a poolside barbeque.
- The decorations may be as simple as a few helium balloons and crepe paper streamers, to no decorations at all, especially if you're planning a clambake on the beach.
- Your music can be anything from recorded music, to a single guitarist, to no music at all.
- Only two elements are required at any wedding reception: a wedding cake and a toast by the best man. Other than that, anything goes.

The good news about any wedding reception, whether formal or not, is that, at the end of the day, you're man and wife. And while your guests will wake up the next morning and go to work as usual, you'll be off on your honeymoon!

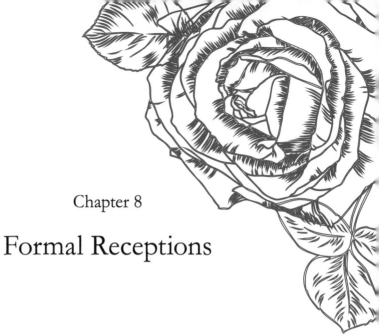

Chapter 8

Formal Receptions

A wedding reception is a joyous affair that celebrates your marriage. An ultraformal or formal wedding reception is more complicated and expensive to plan than a ceremony. In fact, a wedding reception typically accounts for 50 percent of your wedding's total budget. That means that if you have a budget of $26,000, your reception will probably cost around $13,000.

The biggest difference between a formal wedding reception and an informal reception is that the more formal, the more important it is to follow proper etiquette. For example, an ultraformal affair must follow extremely strict rules, such as the precise structure of a receiving line, whereas an informal wedding reception may dispense with the receiving line altogether.

Your first step is to locate a venue suitable to the size and formality of your reception. As you begin your search, you may find that your favorite venues are already booked, which may result in adjusting your wedding date according to when your favorite venue is available. An ultraformal wedding reception usually requires that you book an upscale venue, such as a resort, country club, or hotel ballroom.

An important consideration when selecting your reception venue is whether you will be required to order your food, drink, and wedding cake from it. For example, most restaurants, hotels, and resorts will not allow you to bring in your own caterer or provide your own wedding cake or champagne. However, other venues, such as historical sites, museums, and other city, or county facilities, will allow you to have total control. This means you can save money by shopping around for an affordable caterer, providing some of the food yourself, or purchasing your champagne by the case from Costco or other wholesale warehouse.

Order of the Reception

A typical wedding reception lasts about three hours. If your reception is scheduled to begin at 2 p.m., this is a workable timetable:

2 p.m.   The master of ceremonies announces the members of the bridal party as they walk through the entrance of the reception venue, with the bride and groom the last to enter. If you plan on having a receiving line, it's usually formed immediately. It's proper to have beverages and hors d'oeuvres tray-served by wait staff to the guests as they stand in line.

2:40 p.m. The clergyman or reception host asks a blessing on the meal.

2:45 p.m. The bridal party is seated at the bride's table where they are served by wait staff, as the guests line up for the buffet or are also served a sit-down meal.

3:30 p.m. After everyone has eaten, the musicians play for the couple's first dance, followed by other traditional pairings, and finally by the rest of the guests.

4:00 p.m. The musicians stop playing as the best man offers the first toast, followed by other toasts.

4:15 p.m. After the toasts, the best man or the reception host invites the guests to gather around the cake table for the cake-cutting ceremony. The cake is then served to the guests.

4:30 p.m. Time for the bride's bouquet toss, followed by the groom's garter toss.

4:45 p.m. The bride and groom slip away to change into their traveling attire, while the musicians continue to play and, hopefully, the guests continue to dance, visit, and enjoy themselves.

5:00 p.m.   The best man or reception host makes an announcement that the bride and groom are leaving, and to assemble in the rose garden (or wherever the couple will appear). The bride and groom dash through a shower of bird seed, rose petals, or bubbles, tossed or blown over their heads by the wedding guests as the couple jumps into their getaway vehicle and zooms off on their honeymoon. The guests may return to the reception venue, if they like, for a little more dancing and socializing. However, if you want the reception to be over once the couple has left the site, simply ask the musicians to stop playing.

||||||||||||||||||||||||||||||||||||||||||||||||||||||||||||||||||||||||||||||||||||||||||||||||||||||||

Etiquette 101

In years past, it has been considered poor etiquette for the couple to stay too long at the reception; however, contemporary etiquette allows them to stay as long as they want.

||||||||||||||||||||||||||||||||||||||||||||||||||||||||||||||||||||||||||||||||||||||||||||||||||||||||

According to traditional etiquette, you're only *required* to serve a sit-down or buffet meal if your reception takes place during a regular meal-time. However, an ultraformal or formal reception is usually scheduled to include an upscale lunch or dinner, where a sit-down, plated meal is served. Otherwise, these are the guidelines:

9 a.m. to 11 a.m.   A full breakfast or breakfast buffet.

11 a.m. to 1 p.m.   A brunch buffet.

Noon to 2 p.m.   Sit-down or buffet-style luncheon.

2 p.m. to 5 p.m.   Tea reception with hors d'oeuvres or tea sandwiches.

4 p.m. to 7 p.m.   Cocktail reception with hors d'oeuvres and appetizers.

7 p.m. to 9 p.m.   Sit-down or buffet-style dinner reception.

Receiving Line

A receiving line is required for an ultraformal or formal wedding reception. Allow 30 to 40 minutes for every 100 guests. If you have more than 200 guests, you can speed things up by limiting the receiving line to only the bride, groom, and both mothers.

Traditional order

The traditional order of the receiving line is as follows:

* Mother of the bride.
* Father of the bride.
* Mother of the groom.
* Father of the groom.
* Bride.
* Groom.
* Maid or matron of honor.
* Bridesmaids.

According to rules of etiquette, the fathers may opt out of the receiving line. This is a good way to speed things up. If the fathers do opt out, they should spend time socializing with the guests who are not queued up to go through the receiving line. If the bride's or groom's parents are divorced and have not remarried, the fathers should sit out altogether. This eliminates the awkward situation where a divorced couple must stand in the line together.

If parents have remarried and you would like to incorporate stepparents into the receiving line, this is the order, if the bride's father has divorced and remarried:

* Bride's mother.
* Groom's father.
* Groom's mother.
* Bride.
* Groom.
* Bride's stepmother.
* Bride's father.

Theme

The theme of your reception may follow that of the ceremony, or it may have its own personality altogether. Today's most popular themes are described in Chapter 4, including a Victorian wedding, a black and white wedding, and an all-white wedding, also known as a snowball wedding.

Also, each year a certain color becomes popular. One year it may be purple—all shades of purple, with the most popular accent color being lime green, for example.

And finally, according to *www.ezinearticles.com*, three of the most popular themes currently are:

1. Fairy tale themes (such as Snow White or Cinderella and Prince Charming).
2. Beach themes (such as a tropical paradise).
3. Seasonal themes (such as winter, spring, summer, and fall).

Any of these themes may be taken to the limit when planning an upscale reception. For example, a fairy tale wedding may include a glass carriage or a castle ice sculpture.

Once you've chosen your theme, ask your wedding coordinator to help incorporate it into every element of your reception, from the flowers to the site décor, to the lighting and the music. Of course, the earlier you choose your theme, the easier it will be for your coordinator, floral designer, and the rest of your service providers.

Flowers

The more formal your reception, the larger and more elaborate the floral decorations should be. (Remember that floral arrangements should be higher or lower than the eye-level of the guests. Otherwise, they may interfere with the guests' conversations.) An ultraformal or formal reception may include some of these options:

- A large, exquisite floral centerpiece for the bride's table.
- Smaller, yet elegant, arrangements for the guest tables.
- Arbors and arches decorated with greenery, ribbon, and fresh flowers.
- Decorated topiary trees.

- Fresh flowers to adorn the wedding cake and/or the cake table.
- Small flowers attached to the place cards.
- Tall, free-standing floral arrangements framing doorways and the cake table.
- Garlands of greenery, ribbon, and fresh flowers intertwined in and around food displays on the buffet table or the food stations, and draped over doorways and windows.

Site Décor

In addition to the floral displays, the rest or your decorations should be comparable to their degree of formality. Here are popular options:

- Tall, tapered candles or floating votive candles.
- Gold, brass, or silver candelabras.
- Lots of tulle, lace, and ribbon, tied into bows, trailed along the tables or clustered around candles or centerpieces.
- Strings of tiny white lights, draped around indoor plants and floral displays, outdoor trees, and bushes.
- Paper lanterns.
- Decorative screens.
- Rented statuary.
- White or wrought iron benches.
- Carousel horses.
- Ice sculptures.

Table Décor

If an ultraformal or formal reception, your tables should be decorated according to your reception theme and wedding colors. For example, if your colors are raspberry and pale pink, cover the tables with matching linen cloths and napkins, and place complementary floral arrangements on each table. Gold or silver candlesticks with long tapered candles add an elegant touch.

||||||||||||||||||||||||||||||||||||||||||||||||||||||||||||||||||||||||||||||||||||||||||||||||||||

Etiquette 101

Be sensitive to the dietary restrictions of your friends, family members, and guests. For example, ask the caterer to include a vegetarian dish, plus kosher foods if it is an interfaith wedding where the bride or groom is Jewish.

||||||||||||||||||||||||||||||||||||||||||||||||||||||||||||||||||||||||||||||||||||||||||||||||||||

Wedding Favors

Traditional wedding favors are small gifts given to the women and girls present, although many favors today are given to all the guests. At an ultraformal or formal reception, you often find pricey favors, such as Godiva chocolates, sterling silver framed photos of the bride and groom, or wine bottles with personalized labels that include the couple's names and wedding date.

Reception Seating

When guests are seated around tables, it's considered proper etiquette to provide place cards, so the guests will know where to sit. If you don't provide a place card for each guest, assign someone the task of informing your guests where they are to be seated as they arrive at the reception venue. This can be easily accomplished by making up an alphabetical guest list ahead of time with a table number beside each name. If you choose this option, be sure the table numbers are tall enough to be seen by the guests as they scan the room.

In addition to the guests' tables, there should be a head table, sometimes called the bride's table, where the bride and groom are seated along with the members of their wedding party. The bride and groom sit at the center of the table, the best man beside the bride, and the bride's honor attendant beside the groom. The groomsmen and the bridesmaids sit alternately—boy, girl, boy, girl—on each side of the best man and the bride's honor attendant.

The bride's table is usually one long rectangular table with everyone seated on one side facing the guests. In the case of an exceptionally large wedding party, the bride's table may be arranged in a U-shape, with the opening of the U facing the guests. A round bride's table is also popular because the wedding party can see each other and easily carry on a conversation.

If your wedding party is small, you may include each attendant's spouse or date at the head table. Otherwise, the spouses and dates may be seated together at a table as close as possible to the head table.

Other tables should be designated for the couple's parents, grandparents, and other relatives, especially those who have traveled from out of town. The parents' table should include both sets of parents, plus the officiant and his or her spouse. If your parents are divorced, or divorced and remarried, seat them at separate tables with relatives from their sides of the family. Also, take care to separate feuding friends or relatives, assigning them to tables as far apart as possible.

Give careful thought to the seating of the rest of your guests as well, clustering them in groups according to their ages and interests. It's a good idea to involve both mothers in this planning. Here are a few helpful suggestions:

- Designate a table for out-of-town relatives who haven't seen each other in quite a while and want to visit.

- Designate one or more tables for single adults.

- When seating couples, always alternate the men and women around the tables, keeping the couples separated.

- Seat older guests as far from the music as possible.

The Bride's Cake Table

A special table is provided for the wedding cake, or more properly called, "the bride's cake." The wedding cake is one of the two required elements for any wedding reception. (The second required element is a toast by the best man.) It should be large enough to serve every guest who would like a piece. It should be noted, however, that not all guests will eat cake at all, for any number of reasons—they're diabetic, on a diet, too full from eating the reception meal, or, believe it or not, some people don't *like* cake!

The cake table may be decorated with flowers, and it may also provide mints, along with small plates upon which the cake will be served. The bridesmaids' bouquets may be placed on the cake table as decorations, arranged around the front of the table, facing the guests.

The cake cutting ceremony is an important element of the reception. This is the traditional cake-cutting sequence:

- The groom should place his right hand over the bride's right hand as they cut into the bottom layer. Then, they feed bites of cake to each other.

- After you have fed each other, you should each cut and serve individual slices of cake to your respective in-laws, the bride serving the groom's parents, and vice versa.

- After this, someone else may continue with the cake cutting, such as a friend of the bride, or a member of the catering staff. When the bottom layer has been served, the next layer up is cut in the same way, from the outside in to where the next layer begins. This same sequence is followed until the top layer has been reached.

- The top layer is often saved, frozen, and brought out to be served during the couple's first anniversary celebration. If you choose this option, the cake will need to be triple-wrapped and placed in freezer bags, or it won't last a year.

|||||||||||||||||||||||||||||||||||||||||||||||||||||||||||||||||||||||||||||||||||||||||||||||||||||||||||||

Etiquette 101

The cake smash is one of my least favorite things. Not only is it terrible etiquette, but it just seems silly to smash cake into each other's faces after spending so much money on an elegant affair. You can take this with a grain of salt, but if I had my way there would never be another cake smash.

|||||||||||||||||||||||||||||||||||||||||||||||||||||||||||||||||||||||||||||||||||||||||||||||||||||||||||||

The Fairmont cake presentation

Many formal wedding receptions, especially evening affairs, provide a dramatic Fairmont cake presentation. This is a presentation where the venue is darkened and the cake, which has been kept hidden, is dramatically spotlighted as it is rolled into the reception venue. There's usually a drum roll, or the band may play a loud fanfare, such as "Here Comes the Bride." Sparklers are often inserted into the top of the cake and lighted just before the cake is rolled out, creating a spectacular show.

The Groom's Cake Table

A groom's cake is usually a dark cake, such as chocolate or fruitcake.

According to strict, traditional etiquette, this cake is cut, boxed up, and presented to each single woman present, which she places under her pillow that night, hoping to dream of the man she's to marry. According to contemporary etiquette, however, the cake may be cut and served during the reception, along with the bride's cake. Or, the cake may be cut and boxed ahead of time to be presented as wedding favors to the guests as they leave the reception. If you decide to cut the groom's cake and serve it during the reception, it should be cut *after* the bride's cake. Whether you cut it up and box it ahead of time, or serve it during the reception, be sure to save the top layer, or at least a piece of the cake, to be frozen and brought out on your first wedding anniversary.

A popular twist is for the groom's cake to symbolize his hobby. For example, if he's a football fan, the cake may be in the shape of a football, with icing "laces." Or, if he's into soccer, it may be in the shape of a soccer ball.

Master of Ceremonies

The bride's father or the groom's best man usually serves as the master of ceremonies. Or, you may have a couple who offers to serve as host and hostess of the reception. Another option is for the bandleader to assume this role.

If the bride's father is the official host, he should welcome the guests as soon as everyone has arrived at the reception venue and gone through the receiving line. By "official host," I mean the person whose name appears at the top of the wedding invitation, which, according to traditional etiquette, is the person hosting the reception. In addition to welcoming the guests, the host, whoever he is, also announces the best man's toast, the beginning of the cake-cutting ceremony, the bouquet toss, and the couple's departure.

In general, the host should see that everything flows according to schedule, so that the reception ends at the designated time. To accomplish this task, he should furnish copies of the planned timetable ahead of time to the best man, musicians, caterers, photographer, and videographer.

||||||||||||||||||||||||||||||||||||||||||||||||||||||||||||||||||||||||||||||||||||||||||||||||||||||||||||||||

Etiquette 101

Preferably the reception host or master of ceremonies should not be a loud, obnoxious person who dominates the affair. I'm sure you've seen this type of character—one of those people who loves to hog the microphone and constantly ham it up. The master of ceremonies's job description is to make announcements and keep things moving along on schedule, using a moderated voice, sans the stand-up comedy routine.

||||||||||||||||||||||||||||||||||||||||||||||||||||||||||||||||||||||||||||||||||||||||||||||||||||||||||||||||

Guest Books

You can provide two guest books, usually placed on a table near the entrance to the reception venue. These books are attended by friends who are dressed in attire complementary to the wedding colors. They wear a corsage or boutonniere.

Wedding Gifts

Traditional etiquette requires that all wedding gifts be delivered to the bride's home before the wedding day. However, in this day of contemporary etiquette, this rule is rarely followed, and so it's common for guests to show up with gift in hand. Also, certain cultures and ethnic groups expect the guests to bring their gifts to the reception. In any case, you'll need to provide an attractively decorated gift table where the gifts may be placed.

Provide a decorated box with a slit in the top for wedding cards, especially those that may contain cash or a check. It's a good idea to provide paid security, or have a trusted friend keep an eye on gifts and the card box. Ask the security officer or friend to tape any cards to their corresponding gifts. Unfortunately, there are well-dressed thieves who specialize in crashing wedding receptions unnoticed and walking away with gifts or the card box.

By the way, it's poor etiquette to open wedding gifts during the reception. It's also in poor taste to display previously opened gifts. The exception to this rule is when certain cultures traditionally display all wedding gifts at the reception, including gifts received before the wedding. Traditional etiquette expected all wedding gifts be delivered to the bride's home or her parents' home where they were opened and placed in an attractive display. This tradition still takes place in the South.

Music

When planning an ultraformal or formal wedding reception, you should provide live music, such as one or two bands, or an orchestra to play in a formal ballroom. A daytime wedding that doesn't require dancing, such as a brunch or tea reception, may require only one or two musicians to play background music. For example, you may hire a harpist or pianist to play classical selections. You may also provide specialty musicians, such as a bagpiper.

||||||||||||||||||||||||||||||||||||||||||||||||||||||||||||||||||||||||||||||||||||||||||||||||||||||||||||||||||||||||||||

Etiquette 101
Your wedding reception is not a live concert, so keep the volume down so guests can socialize with each other as they dance or listen to the music.

||||||||||||||||||||||||||||||||||||||||||||||||||||||||||||||||||||||||||||||||||||||||||||||||||||||||||||||||||||||||||||

Dance order

This is the traditional dance order for a wedding reception:
- The bride and groom dance the first dance, usually to their favorite song.
- The bride dances with her father.
- The groom dances with his mother.
- The bride dances with her new father-in-law, and the groom dances with his new mother-in-law.
- The bride dances with the best man, and the groom dances with the bride's honor attendant.
- The bridesmaids and groomsmen join in dancing with each other. If there is an uneven number of bridesmaids and groomsmen, the odd man or woman out may dance with his or her spouse or date.
- All the guests join those already dancing.

Bride and groom's first dance

Here are favorite musical selections:

- "All I Ask of You" from "The Phantom of the Opera" (Webber, Hart, and Stilgoe)
- "Annie's Song" (John Denver)
- "Beautiful in My Eyes" (Joshua Kadison)
- "Because You Love Me" (Celine Dion)
- "Can You Feel the Love Tonight?" (Theme from the *Lion King* by Elton John and Tim Rice)
- "Could I Have this Dance?" (Holyfield and House)
- "Endless Love" (Diana Ross and Lionel Richie)
- "Grow Old With Me" (Mary Chapin Carpenter)
- "My Heart Will Go On" (Theme from Titanic by James Horner and Will Jennings)
- "The First Time Ever I Saw Your Face" (Ewan MacColl)
- "Tonight I Celebrate My Love for You" (Masser and Goffin)
- "You Are So Beautiful" (Fisher and Preston)

Father/daughter dance

Here are favorite musical selections:

- "Butterfly Kisses" (Bob Carlisle)
- "Daddy's Little Girl" (Al Martino)
- "My Heart Belongs to Daddy" (Cole Porter)
- "Thank Heaven for Little Girls" (from Gigi, Lerner, and Lowe)
- "You Are So Beautiful" (Fisher and Preston)

|||||||||||||||||||||||||||||||||||||||||||||||||||||||||||||||||||||||||||||||||||||||||||

Etiquette 101

If the bride is close to both her father and stepfather, one of the fathers may begin the father/daughter dance, then the other cuts in.

|||||||||||||||||||||||||||||||||||||||||||||||||||||||||||||||||||||||||||||||||||||||||||

Mother/son dance

Here are favorite musical selections:

- "I Wish You Love" (Wilson and Tenet)
- "My Mother's Eyes" (Gilbert and Baer)
- "Wind Beneath My Wings" (Silbar and Henley)
- "You Are the Sunshine of My Life" (Stevie Wonder)

Photographer and Videographer

Your photographer and videographer should be as unobtrusive as possible, capturing poignant, candid moments with as many close-ups of the bride and groom as they can get—for example, the couple's faces during their first dance, the bride as she bends to hug her grandmother, or the groom as he embraces his brother after his brother has delivered the best man's toast.

The videographer may also include interviews with several members of the wedding party, plus family members and guests, asking open-ended questions, such as, "When did you first meet the groom?" or "How does it make you feel to be losing your little girl today?"

Traditional posed shots will be on the menu for the photographer as well, including the cake-cutting ceremony and the tossing of the bouquet and garter.

Toasts

The best man's toast is the only one that's required at a wedding reception, although toasts may also be offered by the fathers, the bride and groom, the bride's honor attendant, and other friends and relatives.

Toasts are offered once all the guests have been served a toasting beverage, whether with a meal or, if no meal is served, with the wedding cake. The toasting beverage is poured in this order:

1. Bride.
2. Groom.
3. Maid or matron of honor.
4. All the other guests at the head table, with the best man being served last.

The best man offers the first toast, followed by the fathers, the groom, the bride, friends, relatives, maid or matron of honor, the mothers, and anyone else who would like to propose a toast. Wedding toasts are usually made to the bride or groom individually, the bride and groom as a couple, the bridesmaids, the bride's parents, and the guests. If you're the one being toasted, stay seated and *never* raise your glass or drink from it during the toast itself. It is safe to take a sip, however, once everyone else has done so.

Always stand when offering a toast; the person or persons being toasted should remain seated. Never tap on a glass with a spoon or fork to garner guests' attention. This is in extremely poor taste. The best man has the option of offering his toast before the meal is eaten, but if he does so, he must be sure everyone has been served a toasting beverage. Examples of wedding toasts follow.

Toasts from the best man to the bride and groom

What an honor to be here, [couple's names], to be able to share the joy of this day with you as [groom's name]'s, best man. You know, when [groom's name] was in high school and college, he didn't date very much, as least not that I knew. He was very selective—preferring to spend his time on the basketball court, or cruising over to the coast in his restored '56 Chevy. Rather than dating someone who didn't meet his high standards, he rarely dated at all.

Then he met you [bride's name], and he was a goner. No more hours on the basketball court, and his cruisin' days were over...and why? Because there was nothing he'd rather be doing than spending time with you. You were the one! In fact, it couldn't be more obvious to everyone in this room that you were meant for each other. As you set off together as partners on this journey called marriage, may every day be as joyous as this. Here's to you, [couple's name].

As [groom's name]'s best man, please join me in a toast to our newlyweds. Actually, I have no idea why I'm called the 'best man' because, as far as I know, no one pays the least bit of attention to a man in my position. You hear comments such as: 'Isn't the bride absolutely radiant?' or 'Isn't the groom handsome?' But do you ever hear anyone say, 'Wow, have you noticed the best man—isn't he a great looking guy?' Nooooooooo. In fact, one of the guests thought I was with [name of the catering service]. Actually, I want you all to know that I've been an outstanding best man. Who else could have calmed [groom's name] nerves the way I did? Who else could have been such a wise counselor? Who else could have been such a reassuring voice in his ear as I stood beside him during the ceremony? And who else could have done such an awesome job of arranging the honeymoon, and keeping their honeymoon destination such a fine secret, I might add?

Actually, now that I think about it, with such outstanding qualities as these, I can't help wonder why I'm still single. But seriously, it has been an honor to serve as [groom's name] best man, and it is a special privilege to offer the first toast to the bride and groom. Here's to [couple's names].

I would like to propose the first toast to [couple's names], I've never seen you happier than you are today, and it's all because of this amazing woman sitting next to you. [Bride's name], thank you for making my friend so happy. Please raise your glasses and join me in a toast to a lifetime of happiness for [couple's names].

A toast from the best man to the bridesmaids (on behalf of the bride and groom)

Ladies and gentlemen, it is now my pleasure to propose a toast of thanks and good wishes to the bridesmaids, not only on my behalf, but on behalf of the bride and groom. Your beauty brightened the ceremony, and your flawless performance enhanced the service with a lovely dignity. To the bridesmaids!

A toast on behalf of the bridesmaids (in reply to the bride's and groom's "thank you" toast to the bridesmaids)

On behalf of the bridesmaids, I raise my glass in a toast of thanks to [couple's names] for the kind words they expressed to the bridesmaids. [Groom's name] was so preoccupied with his beautiful bride, I'm surprised he even noticed the brides-maids, much less how lovely they all looked in their [color the bridesmaids' gowns] gowns. Actually, I was enormously impressed with their contribution to the cer-emony—of course, I'm still a bachelor, so my thinking may be a bit skewed, but as they preceded the bride down the aisle, I don't think I've ever seen a more stunning parade of women in my life, On their behalf, I thank you.

Traditional toasts to the bride

Ladies and gentlemen, please stand with me as we join in the traditional toast to the bride: health, happiness, and all the best life has to offer. To [bride's name].

[Bride's name], there was never a bride more beautiful and radiant than you are today. Best wishes for a joyous married life, full of good health and happiness.

Traditional toasts to the bride and groom

Ladies and gentlemen, please stand with me as we raise our glasses in a toast to the bride and groom. [Couple's names], we wish you a lifetime of health and happiness.

Please stand and join me in this traditional toast to the bride and groom. May the most you ever wish for be the least you ever receive.

Contemporary toasts to the bride and groom

I would like to propose a toast to [couple's names]. Your ceremony was filled with some of the most beautiful music I've ever heard. My wish for you is that your marriage will be as melodic and harmonious as the music we heard today. May the music of your love overcome any discords that come your way. To a life-time of joy and harmony.

Please join me as we toast [couple's names]. May your life together be filled with joy, bathed in loved, and nourished by each other's care.

[Couple's names], today is the first day of the rest of your life, a life filled with joy and adventure as your love encompasses every aspect of every day. Your part-nership will be amazing. Every one of us here who knows you as individuals can't wait to see what you accomplish together as a team. We promise to encourage you and support you along the way, and we'll always be there for you when you need us. To [couple's names].

I would like to propose a toast to our lovely couple—may the joy of your love grow deeper with each hour; may your friendship grow closer each day; and may your marriage grow richer each and every year. I love you both. Cheers!

May you have warm words on a cold evening,
A full moon on a dark night.
May the roof above you never fall in,
And the friends gathered below never fall out.
May you never be in want,
And always have a soft pillow for your head.
May you be 40 years in heaven,
Before the devil knows you're dead.

May you be poor in misfortunes, rich in blessings.
Slow to make enemies and quick to make friends.
But be you rich or poor, quick or slow,
May you know nothing but happiness from this day forward.
(A traditional Irish wedding toast to the couple)

Religious toasts to the bride and groom

Please stand with me as we honor [couple's names]. May your love for each other always be a reflection of the perfect love of Christ for His church. We wish you true peace and happiness through Him all the days of your married lives together. To [couple's names].

I would like to propose a toast to our newlyweds, [couple's names]. What an incredible wedding day this is. It is a day unlike any other; no ordinary day, this day, but a day that brings you together in God's divine providence; no ordinary flowers, these flowers, but flowers whose scents waft over us, sweet reminders of the beautiful world He has created for us; no ordinary rings, these rings, but rings that form never-ending circles, sweet reminders of your never-ending love; and finally, no ordinary vows, your vows, those promises made from your innermost hearts, sweet reminders of your never-ending commitment to each other. God bless our newlyweds.

To [couple's names]. May God hold you always in the hollow of His hand.

Toasts by the father of the bride

[Bride's mother's name] and I would like to welcome you all here today and tell you how pleased we are to see our daughter looking so happy. Of course, we have lost a daughter today, but we entrust her to [groom's name] care without reservation, knowing how much he loves her and wants only the best for her. We've gotten to know [groom's name] well over the last few months, and we're convinced he's the right man for [bride's name]. He has all the attributes we could have hoped for, and more. He's an honest, sincere man of integrity, charming, reliable—what can we say? He just couldn't be a greater guy! I know you all agree, so please stand with me as we wish them a happily married life together. To [couple's names].

[Couple's names], there are no words to adequately express the happiness and exhilaration we feel in our hearts today. [Bride's mother's name] and I are absolutely overjoyed with your marriage, and if you two can be even half as happy as we have been, you'll have it made. [couple's names], here's to a lifetime of happiness.

Toasts by the father of the groom

It has been said that when children find true love, parents find true joy. [Couple's names], you have certainly found true love, that kind of lasting love that makes a marriage a joy, the kind of love [groom's mother's name) and I have had for more than [number] years. Thank you for the joy you have brought us by the joining of your hearts and lives together this day. Here's to my son and his beautiful wife.

There is an old English proverb that states: 'A joy that's shared is a joy made double.' [Groom's name], your Mom and I are so happy for you and [bride's name], and may your joy be doubled as you leave here today to begin your new life together as husband and wife. To [couple's names].

A toast by the father of the groom to the bride's parents

I would like to take this opportunity to thank [bride's parents' names]. You have been charming, gracious hosts and it is an honor to be related to you through the marriage of our children. I hope our friendship continues to grow through the years, and I know it will. Here's to [bride's parents' names].

A toast by the groom to his bride

I would like to propose a toast to my bride, [bride's name]. With this toast, I pass all my love from my heart to yours.

As I lift this glass in a toast to my beautiful bride, we see that the glass is full. There may be times in our future, [bride's name], when the glass is only half full, but when those times come, and they will, may the empty space be merely an opening, an opportunity to fill our lives with even greater hope. To our glorious future together as husband and wife. May our lives always be filled with joy even when our glasses are only half-full. To my bride!

I was told ahead of time that you were the most beautiful bride anyone had ever seen, but I was blown away when I saw you walking down the aisle on your

Dad's arm. I agree, you are the most beautiful, and I can't wait to love you, take care of you, and spend the rest of my life with you. To my bride!

Religious toasts by the groom to his bride

The Bible says that it is not good for a man to be alone, and how I praise God for bringing you to me. Before you came into my life, I thought I was self-sufficient—and doing quite well, actually—but now I know that without you I was a mere shadow of the man God really wants me to be. [Bride's name], not only are you my best friend, but my strength and my inspiration—the power that propels my spirit day by day. You have filled a void in my life that I didn't even know existed. To my wife--the wind beneath my wings.

Here's a toast to my bride, [bride's name], and to a lifetime of loving and serving each other, just as our hearts long to love and serve God. To my bride.

I would like to propose a toast to my bride. May we each be shelter to the other; may we each be warmth to the other; and may our days be good and long upon this earth. (Inspired by an Apache prayer)

I would like to propose a toast to my bride, [bride's name]. Our God has created us as bride and bridegroom, and because of Him, we rejoice. May our marriage always be a testimony to His love and providence. (A Jewish toast)

A thank-you toast by the groom to the bride's parents

I would like to propose a toast to [bride's parents' names]. You have raised quite a daughter here (smiles at his wife.) Thank you for entrusting her to me—I will do my best not to disappoint you. Thank you for accepting me into your family as your son, and for providing us with such a memorable wedding day. We love you! To [bride's parents' names].

A thank-you toast by the groom to his parents

I would like to propose a toast to my parents. Mom and Dad, although it's really difficult for me to put my feelings into words, I want you to know how much I appreciate your love and encouragement through the years. You've made a lot of sacrifices for me—especially when I was struggling to get through college—and I'll never forget it. You're the best parents a son could ever have, and you've set a wonderful example for me of what a really good marriage should be. Thank you for helping make our wedding day so special. To my Mom and Dad.

A religious toast from the bride or groom to their parents

I would like to propose a toast to my parents. Mom and Dad, thank you for raising me in a Christian home with Christian values. Because of you I have a strong faith in God, a solid foundation for life and for marriage. No child could receive a more precious legacy than that. I love you both.

A toast by the bride to her groom

For all the wonderful ways you've touched my heart, and for all the unexpected ways you've changed my life, I love you. To my husband.

[Groom's name], I will always remember the first time I saw you, the first time you held my hand, the first time you brought me flowers, the first time you kissed me good night. All these memories, and others too, are timeless treasures stored within my heart, to be relished and savored at will. But of all the memories, none can compare with those made here today—the expression on your face as Dad walked me down the aisle, the sound of your voice as you recited your vows, your kiss and your smile. I will remember them until the day I die. To my husband!

Religious toasts by the bride to her groom

I would like to propose a toast to my husband. I know we both believe that our marriage has been sanctioned by God, and I want you to know that I feel blessed beyond measure that He brought you into my life. To my husband.

[Groom's name], in the book of Genesis, Adam said, 'This is now bone of my bones, and flesh of my flesh; she shall be called woman.' Today, as we became joined as husband and wife, we are no longer two individual people, but joined as one. God has willed this, and He has given me to you to be your 'woman' from this day forward. What a lovely plan that is! Thank you, Lord. To my husband.

A toast by the bride to her groom and both sets of parents

I would like to propose a toast to my husband and his parents, who raised him to be the caring, responsible man of integrity he has become. You were always there for [groom's name], supporting him in every way possible. I would like to take this opportunity to thank you publicly for making me feel so loved and such a welcome member of your family. I would also like to toast my parents and to thank them for their love, their support and their prayers. I'm so blessed to have such marvelous parents—and I especially thank you, Mom and Dad, for giving [groom's name] and me such an incredible wedding day. Here's to my husband and to our parents.

A toast by the bride to her bridesmaids

I would like to propose a toast to my bridesmaids. Thank you for making my day so special. I love you all. Here's to [first names of her attendants].

A toast to the bride by her mother

One day you wake up and realize that you've given birth to your best friend. [Bride's name], you truly are my best friend, and my heart is overflowing with my love for you, my precious daughter, on this, the happiest day of your life. I have so much I'd like to say, but mere words are inadequate to express my feelings. As I helped you dress this morning—and what a beautiful bride you are—and helped arrange the veil around your sweet face, I realized that you're not a little girl anymore, but a thoughtful, caring woman with very special dreams, and so much love to give to [groom's name]. I toast you, [bride's name], my cherished daughter and my best friend.

A toast to the bride by her best friend or honor attendant

I would like to propose a toast to [bride's name]. You are the most loving, understanding friend anyone could have. No one cares from the heart like you care, and no one listens from the heart like you do. Thank you for being my 'sister of the soul.' I wish you a beautiful life with [groom's name]. To my best friend, [bride's name].

Tossing of the Bouquet

The bride tosses her bouquet backward over her head to a group of single women. The one who catches it is said to be the next to marry. Most brides prefer to keep and preserve their bridal bouquet, so they toss a less expensive version of the bouquet to the women. Another option is to dispense with this tradition entirely, or present the bouquet to the bride's mother, grandmother, or the woman present who has been married the longest.

Tossing of the Garter

The bride or her groom removes a garter from her thigh, which the groom tosses backward over his head to a group of single men. The one who catches it is said to be the next to marry. Many couples are dispensing with this tradition.

The Couple's Getaway

Traditionally, guests have showered the bride and groom with rice as they make their getaway; however, many venues don't allow rice, which has resulted in lovely new customs, such as ringing the church bells, releasing love doves or helium balloons, tossing rose petals, blowing bubbles, or waving lighted sparklers.

Chapter 9

Informal Receptions

An informal wedding reception has fewer restrictions than an ultraformal or formal reception. Gone are all those pesky rules of etiquette, such as the precise structure for your receiving line, required for a formal or ultraformal reception. At your informal reception, you don't even need a receiving line.

Two requirements still exist for every reception, however: a wedding cake and a toast to the couple by the best man; other than that, anything goes. Here are options for each element of your informal reception:

Venue

An informal wedding reception can take place anywhere, such as:

- A park.
- Ranch/barn.
- Grandma's backyard.
- High-rise rooftop.
- Church's social hall.
- Community center.
- Elk's Club hall.
- A public or private garden.
- Around a swimming pool.
- Bed and breakfast.
- Winery.

- On a beach.
- Art gallery.
- Ferryboat.

Flowers

If an informal reception, all you need is a small floral centerpiece for the head table, if you have one, and one for each guest table. These flowers can be as simple as clusters of lilacs from Grandma's garden, or old wine bottles filled with wild flowers. You can also bring the floral decorations from the ceremony venue, unless you plan to get married at your reception site, which is customary for a super-casual wedding.

Theme

A theme for an informal or super-casual reception can be as simple as taking advantage of the outdoor ambience, such as a garden or beach; decorating the site in the wedding colors; or incorporating your hobbies. For example, if you both ride Harleys, decorate your bikes and wheel them into the reception venue! A country western theme is ideal for a barn wedding, or bring the country western theme into any venue and decorate with bales of hay, saddles, cowboy hats, and boots. Use your imagination; anything goes!

Table Decor

Same goes for your table decorations—use inexpensive containers for the loose flowers you bring from your garden or a supermarket floral department, and add a few decorative items that fit your theme. For example, back to the country western idea, set the tables with red and white checkered tablecloths, Mason jars as glasses, and pie tins as "plates." Scatter a few Hershey's kisses around the tables as "favors" and you're ready for a barbecue. You can also use disposable paper tablecloths, plastic plates, cups, napkins, and dinnerware.

Wedding Favors

Traditional wedding favors are small gifts given to the women and girls present, although many favors today are given to all the guests. At an informal reception, you may see:

- Packages of flower seeds.
- Decorated boxes filled with candy or cookies.
- Coffee mugs and gourmet coffee beans.
- Jordan almonds wrapped in tulle.
- Small potted flowers or herbs.
- Scratch-off lottery tickets.

Reception Seating

The guests can sit at tables or on chairs placed around the perimeter of the venue. Or, if a pool party reception, for instance, they can sit on the pool deck. No rules apply!

||||||||||||||||||||||||||||||||||||||||||||||||||||||||||||||||||||||||||||||||||||||||||||||||||||||||||||||||||||

Etiquette 101

The best man has the option of offering his toast before the food is served or later on during the wedding reception. The important thing for him to remember is that every guest needs a toasting beverage before he offers his toast, even if it's just a can of beer.

||||||||||||||||||||||||||||||||||||||||||||||||||||||||||||||||||||||||||||||||||||||||||||||||||||||||||||||||||||

Master of Ceremonies

An informal wedding reception doesn't need a designated master of ceremonies; the bride's father or the best man can keep the party going. The only two important announcements are the best man's toast and the cutting of the wedding cake.

Guest Book

You can provide a guest book at your informal reception, or you can substitute a wedding "diary," a blank book where the guests write messages to the bride and groom. The guests may also sign the matting of your engagement photograph, which can be displayed on an easel.

Wedding Gifts

Traditional etiquette requires that all wedding gifts be delivered to the bride's home before the wedding day. However, in this day of contemporary etiquette, this rule is rarely followed, and so it's common for guests to show up with gift in hand, especially during an informal reception. Designate someone to safeguard the gifts and, especially, any gift cards that may contain money or checks.

Food and Drink

You may offer homemade reception food or deli food from the supermarket, served on a buffet-style table, decorated with a single floral arrangement. Or, in the case of a super-casual reception, you'll probably be eating barbecue on the beach or around a pool.

You can provide anything you want: spiked or non-spiked punch, pitchers of cold lemonade, tubs filled with iced beer and soda, or bottles of red and white wine. Whatever you serve, hold some back to be served before the wedding toasts.

Wedding Cake

You must serve a wedding cake, no matter how casual the reception. It doesn't need to be a four-layer cake with an exquisite cake-top, but it needs to be something: a small supermarket sheet cake, a round homemade layer cake, or it can be a novelty cake depicting the reception's theme or the couple's hobbies.

Invite Your Pet to Your Party

Have your pet "offer a toast." Ask someone to lead your dog or cat into the reception venue with an envelope attached to its collar. Then, when it comes time for the toasts, have the best man say something like, "Oh, I see that Brutus wants to offer a toast to his master." Then, the best man removes the card from the envelope and reads the toast, which can be composed ahead of time with cute comments that relate to the bride or groom, such as, "I want to toast my Mommy and my new Daddy. Thank you for letting me come to your wedding. I thought you were going to make me stay in that stupid cage in the kitchen. You look so pretty, Mommy. Glad you picked a guy who likes dogs. I love you."

Include your pet in your reception photos. Although your pet may not participate in the wedding itself, it will still be part of your wedding memories for years to come. If your reception venue allows pets, take interior photos; if not, take exterior photos. For example, a pet horse affords a fantastic photo opportunity—the bride and/or groom can pose atop its back. Then the videographer can catch you riding off together, or your groom leading you on the back of the horse.

Music

For an informal indoor reception, you can provide recorded music or a DJ. If it's a casual reception where you and your guests are gathered around a campfire on the beach, the crashing waves will provide the melodies. If the reception takes place at a country western bar, the band will provide the beat for your line-dancing guests.

Photographer and Videographer

You may hire a photographer and videographer, or, more likely, you'll ask a friend or relative to bring along a camera and camcorder. You can also bring a basket of disposable cameras for your guests to use as they capture the candid moments of your informal reception. Request close-up shots of you and your groom.

Tossing of the Bouquet and Garter

Depending on the formality of your reception, you may dispense with both of these traditions. Otherwise, the bride tosses her bouquet backward over her head to the single women present, and the groom tosses her garter to the single men. Whoever catches the bouquet and garter are said to be the next to marry.

The Couple's Getaway

Depending on your reception's formality, or lack thereof, you can make your getaway in a pickup truck, dad's Lexus, or riding double on the back of your pet horse. In any case, the guests will probably toss bird seed or blow bubbles as you depart.

Toasts

The only required toast is by the best man, toasting the bride and groom. At an informal wedding reception, any guest or family member may offer a toast if they want, and it isn't necessary for the toasts to be worded just so. During an informal reception, the toasts may be impromptu as guests think of something they'd like to say on the spot.

Here are examples of informal toasts:

Toasts from the best man to the bride and groom

Is everyone enjoying themselves? Is this a great occasion, or what? Of course, most of us who know [groom's name] thought this day would never come. We were all sure he was a confirmed bachelor—until he met [bride's name], of course. Actually, you can thank me for that. In fact, I feel like a real matchmaker. You see, I had been nagging at [the groom] to come with me to the gym, just to try it out—you know. I was sure once he got into the fitness thing he'd really like it. Well, after a year of nagging at him, I finally pulled him away from his computer one night and dragged him over to the club. But was he impressed? Not at all. He said he preferred riding his mountain bike and swimming laps. So, admitting defeat, I gave up on him.

Then, the strangest thing happened. Suddenly he decided he liked working out after all, and not only did he join the club, but he was over there four or five nights a week. I couldn't figure it out until I tagged along with him one night and noticed [groom's name] spending most of the time hanging out at the service counter talking to one of the girls who worked there—a gorgeous brunette by the name of [bride's name]. And, of course, we all know what that led to—wedding bells!

So, you have me to thank for this fantastic day! Seriously, [couple's names], I couldn't be happier for both of you. You're a perfect couple, and I'm honored to have served as your matchmaker! Please join me as I toast [couple's names].

I would like to toast [couple's names]. Few things endure through a person's lifetime like the power of friendship, and [groom's name], I value our friendship. You've been that one rare friend in my life who has always been there for me, and we've been through a lot together, haven't we? I remember the time we scrounged around our dorm room hunting for enough loose change to at least buy a loaf of bread and a jar of peanut butter to get us by until the first of the month. And that winter when we went a whole semester with no wheels because neither one of us could afford to get our cars fixed—it's not great bicycling around campus in 20 degree weather.

But looking back on it all, the sacrifices were worth it. We survived those years, and so did our friendship. As you and [bride's name] begin your life together as a married couple, I pledge my continued friendship to both of you—whenever you need me—just holler, and I'll be there. Here's to a lifetime of joy and happiness.

||||||||||||||||||||||||||||||||||||||||||||||||||||||||||||||||||||

[With mock mourning] My dear friends, we are gathered here today to say goodbye to our dearly departed brother, [groom's name], who has left the land of the living for that never-never land known as 'married life.' We tried to warn [groom's name], we told him to be careful or this very thing might happen, but would he listen? Nooooo. We warned him that he'd be forced to give up all those pleasurable rounds of golf, because he'd be repairing the roof or helping his wife clean house. We warned him that he'd have to give up his carefree Saturday afternoons shooting hoops with the guys, because his wife would insist he follow her around as she spent his money at the mall. And, of course, gone were the lazy Sunday afternoons when he could kick back and watch a little football—he would be spending them with his in-laws instead [glances at the bride's parents]. Well, we did the best we could, but he wouldn't listen. For some crazy reason he was convinced that the joys of married life would far outweigh the pleasures of bachelorhood. Can you imagine that?

Seriously, though, all of us who have come to know and love [bride's name] understand his reasoning completely. [Bride's name], you are so perfect for [groom's name], and I know you'll fill his days with more joy and contentment than he could have found in a thousand rounds of golf or a hundred games of one-on-one. [Groom's name], you've finally found the right woman, and we're happy for you. Here's to [couple's names].

||||||||||||||||||||||||||||||||||||||||||||||||||||||||||||||||||||||||||||||||||||||||||||||||||||||||||||||||

Etiquette 101

The best man must always include the bride. Don't get so carried away telling your stories that you neglect to toast the groom *and* the bride.

||||||||||||||||||||||||||||||||||||||||||||||||||||||||||||||||||||||||||||||||||||||||||||||||||||||||||||||||

Informal toast to the bride and groom

What is true love? Lasting love? It's the kind of love we see between [couple's names]. Their love is unselfish, caring, and giving, and they have one of those rare love relationships that touches all our hearts—reminding us of what genuine love should be. [Couple's names], we toast your love, and we wish you joy and happiness in your married life. To [couple's names].

As I toast you, [couple's names] I'd like to suggest a recipe for a happily married life. Take a pound of tenderness. Mix it together with a tablespoon of joy and a cup of laughter. Add a pinch of patience and a sprinkling of kindness. Simmer slowly, watching carefully so that it never comes to a boil. Strain it through a sieve of tolerance, and you'll have a pudding that's not only sweet, but lasting. Please raise your glasses. To [couple's names].

Toasts by the father of the bride

I would like to propose a toast to my daughter. Although it's hard to believe when we see her here today, so elegant and gorgeous in her beautiful wedding gown, with her hair all done up that way and all—she used to be quite a tomboy. Oh, man—did she worry us sometimes. She could climb a tree or ride a horse or play goalie better than half the boys in town, and you loved it, didn't you [bride's name]? Mom would buy you barrettes and ribbons for your hair, hoping you'd doll yourself up a little, but by dinnertime your hair would be back in its braid, fastened with a rubber band. [Groom's name], you never knew her when she was in her tomboy stage, but believe me, there's been quite a transformation. Just look at her—wow! To my beautiful daughter on her wedding day. Thanks for the memories.

[Groom's name], welcome to our family. We've already grown to love you as our own son, and we wish you and [bride's name] a joyous future as you begin your lives as husband and wife. Here's to my new son.

I would like to propose a toast to all of you, our honored guests, and especially to [groom's name]'s family and friends. What a splendid day this has turned out to be—everything has gone so well, even the weather cooperated—such a happy day for all of us. [Bride's mother's name] and I would like to thank you for coming to help us celebrate the marriage of our beautiful daughter and our new son-in-law. We have known quite a number of you for many years, and others we have met for the first time today, but we thank you all for coming. I toast you all!

Toasts by the father of the groom

Our family has always been a circle of strength and love, and with every birth and every union, the circle grows. Every joy shared adds even more love and makes our circle stronger. Thank you, [bride's name] for joining our circle. We welcome you with open arms and, even through we've only known you a short time, we have already grown to love you. We are so happy for both of you. Here's to [couple's names].

———————————————————————

There couldn't be a better time than this to reflect on the pleasures of having a wonderful son like [groom's name]. There have been times through the years when [groom's mother's name] and I looked at each other in wonder. How could we have been so blessed as to have a son like this? [Groom's name], you've done nothing but make us proud—in the choices you've made through the years and the ways you worked so hard to fulfill your goals. You've touched our lives deeply, and it's difficult to find the words to express the love we have for you. And, speaking of choices, you couldn't have chosen a more wonderful woman to be your wife. She's not only beautiful on the outside, but on the inside as well. You've done good, son, and your Mom and I toast you and [bride's name]. May your marriage be filled with as much happiness as you've brought us through the years.

———————————————————————

The father of the groom rises and makes a big show of taking a glass case out of his pocket, unsnapping the case and withdrawing a pair of very dark sunglasses, which he carefully places over his eyes: *Whew! That's better! They say a bride is supposed to be radiant, but this is ridiculous. I have to shield my eyes to look at her. Tell me, have you ever seen a more beautiful bride in your life? And, of course, they say that the groom should beam with happiness. Look at my son. I can feel the glow all the way over here. Truthfully, though (as he removes his sunglasses), you are a beautiful couple, and Mom and I couldn't be happier for you. I toast you, [couple's names] and may your future be filled with the same glowing radiance and incandescent brilliance we see in you here today.*

A toast by the bride or groom to their parents

I would like to propose a toast to my Mom and Dad. Thank you for being such positive role models in my life. I'm proud to be your daughter (or son). You have taught me how to love, to care, and to give. You were always there for me through the years, and I love you for that. Thanks, too, for all the help you've been to [bride or groom's name] and me planning this wedding. Don't think you're getting rid of me, by the way. I plan to be back for Mom's cherry pie [or Dad's homemade ice cream, and so on]. So, save [bride or groom's name] and me a place at the table. We both love you so much.

A toast by the bride or groom to their in-laws

I would like to propose a toast to [groom or bride's name]'s Mom and Dad. Thank you for raising such an incredible man (or woman). I love him/her dearly, and I feel blessed to become part of your family. I hoped to find someone like [groom or bride's name], but I had high ideals, so I wasn't sure anyone like [groom or bride's name] even existed. Then, that day at the association picnic [Fourth of July concert, and so on], I met him/her and I was totally blown away. He/she did exist after all. Thank you for all the help you've given us planning this wedding. We love you very much.

New Year's Eve or Day wedding: A toast for the bride and groom

Here's a toast to [couple's names]. I think this is pretty special—getting married on New Year's Eve—a time for new beginnings. Bless you as you begin your lives as husband and wife, and may all your troubles last as long as my New Year's resolutions.

Valentine's wedding: A toast for the bride and groom

[Couple's names], what a good idea to be married on Valentine's Day—that way you'll never forget your anniversary. Seriously, though, it is fitting to be married on such a day as this, a day set aside for couples in love. To a lifetime of love and happy Valentine's Days!

Christmas Eve or Day wedding: A toast for the bride and groom

[Couple's names], what a lovely day (or evening) to get married, a day (or evening) poignant with the joys of giving and of love as you have given yourselves to each other in the spirit of Christmas. To a future filled with the same love and joy you feel this day (or evening).

Thanksgiving Day wedding: A toast from the groom to his bride

[Bride's name], this is a day of Thanksgiving, and my heart overflows with love for you and thankfulness to have found you. Thank you for giving me a future filled with such hope, happiness, and purpose with you, as my wife by my side.

Thank you for loving and trusting me to care and provide for you all the days of my life. To my bride.

Seaside wedding: A toast for the bride and groom

We toast you, [couple's names]. May your marriage be filled with as many blessings as the grains of sand on this beach. May your love be as deep as this ocean, and your sorrows as light as the foam washing at our feet. To [couple's names].

Garden wedding: A toast for the bride and groom

I hold a beautiful rose (or any other flower may be used). It is perfect and unique. In fact, there is no other rose exactly like it anywhere on earth. [Couple's names], this rose symbolizes the love you have for each other—which is also beautiful and perfect in every way. May each day of your lives be as lovely as this flower. To [couple's names].

Forest wedding: A toast for the bride and groom

We wish you a blessed life together, as fragrant as this forest, as glorious as this sunset, and as tender as a summer shower. May your marriage be filled with sunshine, joy and laughter. To [couple's names].

Waterside wedding: A toast for the bride and groom

Percy Shelley wrote a beautiful poem that fits this moment: "The fountains mingle with the river, and the rivers with the ocean. The winds of heaven mix forever with a sweet emotion; nothing in the world is single, all things by a law divine, in one spirit meet and mingle, why not I with thine?" Indeed we have witnessed today as [couple's names], who have not only met and mingled, but joined together as husband wife. We toast you today and wish you a lifetime of sweet heaven together.

Outdoor winter wedding: A toast for the bride and groom

[Couple's names], we are so blessed to be here with you today to celebrate your marriage. What an idyllic setting this is, with the diamonds sparkling in the snow, the aspen quaking in the breeze, and the sun casting a glow over all. May your marriage be as glorious as this setting, filled with love and beauty for all the years to come. To [couple's names].

Outdoor summer wedding: A toast for the bride and groom

Please stand as we propose a toast to [couple's names]. May your married life together always be as resplendent and idyllic as this place. May your love glow as brightly as the sun shining overhead, and may your troubles be as fleeting as the wispy clouds drifting toward the horizon. To [couple's names].

Celtic wedding: A toast for the bride and groom

I would like to propose a traditional Celtic wedding toast: [Couple's names], "May joy and peace surround you both, and may contentment latch your door. May happiness be with you now and God bless you ever more."

Part 4

After the Wedding

In this section, we'll talk about honeymoons and honeymoon weddings, plus parties and activities that take place after the wedding, including:

- The afterglow party.
- The gift-opening party.
- Mailing of wedding announcements.
- The newspaper announcement.
- Preservation of the bride's gown.

Chapter 10

The Honeymoon

This chapter is divided into two sections, traditional honeymoon and destination wedding. The first section includes options for a traditional honeymoon that follows a home-town wedding. The second section includes options for a destination wedding, where the wedding and honeymoon take place at the same destination.

Traditional Honeymoon

Your first step is to choose a destination. Your second step is to choose your accommodations at that destination. Visit the following Websites to see their top-10 lists of honeymoon destinations: honeymoonersreviewguide. com, tiptoptens.com, travelchannel.com, and honeymoon.about.com.

Favorite Local Honeymoon Destinations

Not every honeymooning couple can afford an exotic destination. Fortunately, there are plenty of romantic options within mainland America. I have done quite a bit of travel writing, and I have found that there are many honeymoon destinations that allow a couple a more local honeymoon. Arizona, for example, offers Tucson, Sedona, and the Grand Canyon. You can visit North Carolina's Outer Banks or South Dakota's Black Hills. California boasts Ft. Bragg–Mendocino, Disneyland, Lake Tahoe, Catalina Island, and San Francisco. Vermont's Lake Champlain and Michigan's Mackinac Island are also great choices. Research your state and its neighbors, and you're sure to find lovely local destinations for your honeymoon.

A Three-Day Honeymoon Weekend

A three-day honeymoon weekend isn't ideal, of course, but often the bride and groom are well established in their careers and can't arrange coinciding vacation days for their honeymoon, so they plan a three-day weekend honeymoon, to be followed by a "real" honeymoon as soon as they find time in the future.

Outdoorsy Honeymoon Destinations

It isn't every couple's dream to spend the days beside a pool or on a beach. Many honeymooners love the outdoors and choose a "sporty" destination. For example, if both of you like to hike and fish, you can find a romantic honeymoon cabin alongside a stream or lake. A couple other ideas for an outdoorsy honeymoon are to rent an RV or a houseboat. Maybe you can spend your winter honeymoon skiing! Also, any national park may also be a good choice. Go online and see what you can find within driving distance of your home town.

A dude ranch may be a great destination for you, especially if you enjoy hunting, fishing, back packing, whitewater rafting, horseback riding, and the rest. Some dude ranches are rather upscale, serving gourmet meals and offering romantic amenities, such as spas and massages. Others are exactly what you would expect them to be: a working ranch, where you help round up cattle, you eat grub off the chuck wagon, and learn how to rope a calf.

||||||||||||||||||||||||||||||||||||||||||||||||||||||||||||||||||||||||||||||||||||||||||||||||||||||||||

Money-Saving Tips

Here are a few money saving tips for your honeymoon:

- Pack plenty of film, batteries, toothpaste, shampoo, and suntan lotion so that you won't need to buy them at your honeymoon destination, where they'll probably be more expensive than your local supermarket.

- Don't even think of touching your hotel room's mini-bar.

- Fill up at your hotel's complimentary breakfast. That way, you'll be less hungry for lunch.

- Avoid taxis as much as possible by using your hotel's free shuttle service or public transportation.

- Order an entertainment book ahead of time for your honeymoon destination, where you'll find two-for-the-price-of-one restaurant meals, plus coupons that will come in handy for tourist attractions.

Destination Wedding

This is a wedding that takes place at your honeymoon destination; it is also known as a travel wedding or a honeymoon wedding. Many couples prefer a destination wedding to a full-blown hometown wedding because:

- It's less expensive.
- It's less complex.
- It's less stressful.
- Guests are limited to your family and members of your wedding party, who pay their own way to the destination.

Here are questions you need to ask before booking your destination wedding through a travel agent:

- What type of travel do you specialize in?
- Have you personally stayed at the resort you are recommending to us?
- Do you have brochures, guidebooks, or videos of the destinations you are recommending?
- How quickly do you return phone calls?
- Do you work full-time or part-time?
- What destinations offer the best deals?
- Will you personally deliver all our paperwork to us at least three weeks before our wedding, including our airline tickets, reservations confirmations, and copy of our travel insurance?
- Can you help us get all the documents (visas, passports, copies of blood tests, or other documents, especially if you're planning a destination wedding) we need for our travel?
- If we have any problems during our travel, will you be available to help resolve the problems? If you're not available at the

moment, can you give us a telephone number of your superior so he or she can help us?

- Do you work closely with independent wedding coordinators at the destinations we are considering for a honeymoon wedding?

- Do you have referrals from other honeymooning couples for whom you have arranged their travel and accommodations?

- Will you work with us to plan a honeymoon that is within our budget?

If your honeymoon wedding destination is within easy driving distance or an inexpensive flight from your home town, you may want to invite a few of your closest friends, especially if they're willing to pay their own way. This happens all the time, especially when the destination is a popular vacation spot, such as Disney World or Las Vegas.

One of the big reasons honeymoon weddings have become popular is that the limited guest list means you don't have to invite everyone at work, your entire church congregation, or everyone you went to school with since kindergarten. When you add up the average per-guest cost of a wedding these days, the money you'll save may pay for your entire destination wedding, with money left over. And, if you *really* want to save money, plan a destination wedding *sans* friends and family. Take advantage of the witnesses provided by your resort, then, when you return, let your parents host a reception if they offer.

Several resorts, especially in Las Vegas, have adopted the latest technology which allows them to stream your wedding live on their Websites. This is an ingenious way for your friends and family to watch your ceremony on their computer screens back home. You can even send wedding invitations, inviting your guests to "watch our wedding online."

Many honeymoon resorts specialize in all-inclusive honeymoon-wedding packages. They provide everything for you at one price, including a wedding consultant. The consultant will explain your options, including:

- Ceremony site.
- Officiant.
- Flowers.
- Photography/videography.
- Wedding meal menus.

- Wedding cake.

- Honeymoon suite.

- Accommodations for your wedding guests.

If you plan to bring your wedding gown with you on the plane, bring it in a hanging bag (do *not* check it through baggage). Make arrangements ahead of time to have wrinkles steamed out at your destination, if necessary.

||||||||||||||||||||||||||||||||||||||||||||||||||||||||||||||||||||||||||||||||||||||||||||||||||||||

What the Groom Needs to Know

If you're booking your bride's airline reservations, be sure to use her *maiden name*. Although she'll be a married woman when she goes through the checkpoints at the airport, all TSA wants to see is that the name on her ticket matches her driver's license.

||||||||||||||||||||||||||||||||||||||||||||||||||||||||||||||||||||||||||||||||||||||||||||||||||||||

Some of the more popular locations for a destination wedding follow:

- Disneyland in California or Disney World in Florida, both of which provide fairy tale weddings, including Cinderella's coach, pulled by white horses. Disney World also offers a combo honeymoon package that includes three or four days at Disney World and a voyage to Disney's private island, Castaway Cay in the Bahamas.

- A cruise ship provides a romantic setting, although, counter to popular belief, most ship captains are not legally authorized to perform a wedding ceremony. Usually, the couple marries on embarkation day while the ship is still docked, or at dockside at one of the cruise ship's ports.

- Las Vegas is a favorite for a honeymoon wedding and can be a relatively inexpensive choice.

- Hilton Head Island.

- San Diego.

- Vail or Breckenridge, Colorado.

- Poconos, Pennsylvania, which are known for their affordable all-inclusive destination wedding packages.

- Mexico, especially Cancun.

- Caribbean islands' couples' resorts, such as Sandals Resorts who offer WeddingMoon packages.

- Hawaii, with its dependable climate year-round and an abundance of romantic venues.

Destination wedding: A toast for the bride and groom

I speak for everyone here when I say that we would go to the ends of the earth to attend your wedding—and it seems we have done exactly that! However, even with the lost luggage, the lousy airline meals, and jet lag, we're all glad we came. Our wish is that your marriage will always be as warm, happy, and glorious as this place. To [couple's names].

Gift baskets

Make arrangements ahead of time for gift baskets to be left in your wedding guests' hotel rooms. Each basket may contain items, such as:

- Handwritten welcome note from the bride and groom.

- Fresh fruit and flowers.

- Schedule of events.

- Disposable camera.

- Bottled water.

- Brochures for local attractions.

- City map.

- If a beach destination, include beach towels, sunscreen, flip-flops, and so on.

Destination weddings in a foreign country

Obtaining a marriage license isn't always easy in a foreign country, and, in fact, it isn't a snap in Hawaii either. Do your homework and determine what documentation and medical tests are required, processing time to obtain a marriage license, and the length of time required between the issuance of the license and the wedding date. For example, you may be required to bring your original birth certificate, your passport, immunization records, copies of blood test results, proof of economic security, or proof that you are free to marry, such as a divorce decree or death certificate, if you were married before. If you're planning a Catholic ceremony in a foreign country, you'll be required to bring your confirmation certificate, baptism certificate, and pre-Cana records. The destination wedding coordinator at your resort should furnish you with all requirements and contact information.

If you will be honeymooning in a foreign country, go to your bank and change some of your money into local currency before you leave. And, oh, yes—keep all your money in a money belt! Not in a wallet. Not in a handbag. A money belt is a little uncomfortable, but worth it.

There are thieves and con artists who take advantage of honeymooners. Here are a few precautions you can take: Watch your luggage carefully. If you're on an airport shuttle, be sure someone doesn't "accidentally" take your luggage with them at their stop. Also, when standing in line at the check-in counter, keep your luggage in front of you, so that they are touching your feet. This will make it more difficult for a thief to walk off with your bags. Also, watch for distractions. For example, a thief may "accidentally" drop his ice cream cone onto your shoulder or lap, then make a big fuss of cleaning you up with a napkin while an accomplice picks your pocket or walks off with your cell phone. Thieves love honeymooners because they know you're probably not paying attention to anyone other than each other.

In order to minimize the risk of lost luggage on your honeymoon: Be sure the bags are tagged with your name, address, and cell phone number, and remove other airline baggage tags before you check your luggage. Make copies of your itinerary and place one inside each piece of luggage, including your carry-ons. Confirm that the three-letter airport code placed on your luggage corresponds with your destination. This is easier to do if you check your luggage curbside.

If, after all your precautions, your luggage gets lost after all, fill out a lost-luggage form with the airline at its customer service desk at your destination airport. Most luggage isn't really "lost," only delayed, and will probably arrive on the next flight. Otherwise, because you were wise and included your itinerary inside your luggage, when it does arrive, the airline will have it delivered to your resort.

Use your favorite social networking site or e-mail to keep your guests apprised of the travel and wedding plans, including schedules, expenses, and so forth. Furnish your guests with brochures provided by the honeymoon destination resort, along with travel brochures for the area.

Here's my final tip for a relaxing honeymoon: when you were planning your wedding, you kept your mobile phone close at all times. After all, your officiant may call with a *very* important question! When you're on your honeymoon, however, put your mobile phone on silent—no vibrating, no nothin'! Take note of any messages you receive from well wishers back home, such as, "Call us and tell us all about your first day in Paris!" But, don't *return* the call—your friends and family will hear all about it when you return. A honeymoon is *not* the time to be answering text messages from work or checking the stock prices. A honeymoon is the time to relax, unwind, and enjoy each other.

Chapter 11

You're Not Done Yet!

After your ceremony and reception, there are more activities, beginning with the afterglow, and ending with the thank-you notes.

Afterglow

An afterglow is an intimate gathering that includes the bride and groom, their immediate families, and any close friends who came from out of town. This get-together follows the reception and is usually hosted by one of the bride or groom's close relatives. It's often held in a private home. A light meal is served. No planning on your part—all you need to do is glow for the guests.

Of course, if you left the reception directly for your honeymoon, you can let them glow over each other, as they re-live the day: how beautiful the bride was as she walked down the aisle, how precious the flower girl was, how poignant the vows were, how the music brought tears to their eyes...

Morning-After Breakfast or Brunch

This can be anything from a formal brunch at a resort, to an informal sausage-and-waffle breakfast in someone's home, usually the home of a close relative or friend. This is where you say your goodbyes before leaving on your honeymoon, if you didn't do so immediately after the reception or the afterglow.

Wedding Announcements

Designate someone to be in charge of mailing your wedding announcements one or two days after the wedding. These announcements go to those who were not invited to the wedding, usually out-of-town friends and relatives. They need to be addressed before the wedding.

Newspaper Announcement

Your wedding announcement should appear in your local newspaper soon after your wedding, unless you delay the announcement so that your wedding photo can be included. Prepare the wording for this announcement before the wedding.

After-the-Honeymoon Gift-Opening Party

The couple's parents often host this party, a casual evening where the bride and groom open their wedding gifts. Only immediate family members and a few close friends are invited.

Preservation of Your Bridal Gown

Your gown should be cleaned and stored as soon as possible after your wedding day. Take it to a dry cleaners that specializes in this type of cleaning and preservation.

What the Groom Needs to Know

You have the option of using a hyphenated version of a surname, combining your surname with your wife's maiden name.

Write the Thank-You Notes

Contrary to popular belief, you do not have a year to write your thank-you notes. Start on them as soon as you return from your honeymoon. Write three or four every day, with a goal to have them all mailed no later than two months after the wedding. It will help if you write as many thank-you notes as possible for gifts received and opened before the wedding.

Here's a brilliant idea: set up a "thank-you note writing center" in your new home before the wedding. Your center should include

- Names and addresses of each donor, along with a description of the gift.
- Stamps.
- Pens with blue or black ink (remember, the thank-yous must be handwritten).
- Wallet-sized wedding photos to enclose in each thank-you note.

This will inspire you to write a few notes every day.

Your thank-you notes must be personalized and written in your own handwriting. It's never acceptable to let someone else help you out by writing thank-you's for you. You would be surprised how many people recognize your mom's or your sister's handwriting!

Here is sample wording:

Dear Aunt Helen,

Thank you for coming to our wedding. Your presence made our day extra special.

Richard and I want to thank you for your thoughtful gift. We love the bread maker. In fact, we've made fresh bread several times. I think Richard is getting spoiled. Thank you so much.

Your loving niece,

Jennifer

It's acceptable to write one thank-you note for a group gift—you don't need to write a separate thank-you note to each member of the group. If you receive money as a wedding gift, take caution when writing your thank-you note. Proper etiquette requires that you don't mention the words "money," "cash," or "check," but refer to it as "your generous gift." Then, add something personal, such as, "Jim and I are putting it toward our new home theater system. Thank you so much," and so on.

The After-Wedding Blues

You've been the center of attention for a year. You've been the guest of honor at half a dozen parties, including the really *big* one, your wedding reception. You've been the center of each other's attention every minute of your glorious honeymoon, perhaps on a cruise ship or at an exotic location, where you were waited on by myriad waiters, resort staff, and poolside attendants.

Now, you're back home and back to work. What a let-down! No wonder newlyweds feel a little depressed for a month or so after all the festivities. You can ease these blues by decompressing slowly: plan a weekend at a bed-and-breakfast on the coast; have friends or family over for your first "company" dinner as a married couple; plan lots of date-nights that not only include dinner, but a concert or theater production. In other words, wear yourself out with activities. This will help you settle down and actually look forward to "a weekend at home alone—finally!"

Part 5

Problem Solving

Problems are inevitable, so when one comes along, don't let it throw you. They range from money problems to personality clashes; from duplicate gifts to inebriated wedding guests.

But don't worry—every problem has a solution. You'll see!

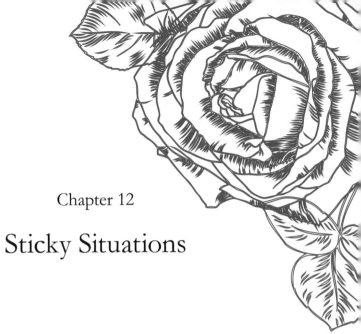

Chapter 12

Sticky Situations

As you plan your wedding, you'll be faced with sticky situations, whether they involve money, gifts, personality clashes, or the unexpected mini-catastrophe. In this chapter you'll find solutions to common problems that may arise.

Money Problems

What happens if the wedding costs escalate and are no longer within our budget?

If you realize your costs are becoming higher than estimated, it's time to re-prioritize. Go over your budget and see which expenses can be cut, if not entirely, at least in their quantity or quality. For example, if the estimated cost of your wedding cake is $650, explore the idea of a supermarket cake instead. You'll be surprised at the high quality and low cost. Or, if your catering costs have skyrocketed, consider asking friends and relatives to supply a few reception food dishes, in lieu of wedding gifts.

My grandparents have decided they can't afford to help us out with our wedding expenses after all. What should we do?

Depending on the dollar amount you were expecting to receive, you may need to make major changes to your spending priorities, such as foregoing the pricey resort reception facilities for your parent's beautifully landscaped back yard.

One of my bridesmaids says she really wants to be in the wedding, but can't afford to purchase airfare or her wedding attire. Do we offer to pay her way?

This is one of the most likely money problems you'll face and, yes, if possible, pay for her airfare and wedding attire. The important thing is to keep it quiet—don't let this news get around to the rest of the bridal party. Consider these expenses part of your wedding budget.

Gift Problems

What happens if we receive duplicate gifts?

This is easily solved. Exchange one of them for something else, but don't let the donors know. Write each a thank-you note, as if their gift was the one-and-only.

What if a gift arrives damaged or broken?

If you know where the gift was purchased, return it for a replacement. However, don't let the donor know the gift arrived damaged, but write a lovely thank-you-note and don't breathe a word about it. Only when a broken or damaged gift arrives fully insured should you contact the donor.

What if we receive a gift we really don't like or want?

You have three options. First option: keep it anyway in case the donor visits your home and wonders why the red and green ceramic rooster isn't perched somewhere in your kitchen. Second option: if you know where it was purchased, exchange for something else. Third option: re-gift it by giving it to someone else in the future. This is a bit risky, however. What if you accidentally give it to the person who gave it to you in the first place?

What happens if the wedding is canceled for some reason? Are we required to return the gifts?

Absolutely. You must return all gifts with a note which may read something like this: "Dear Bob and Ginny, Unfortunately Brad and I have canceled our wedding. We are returning the lovely tablecloth you sent us. Thank you for your thoughtfulness."

‖‖

What the Groom Needs to Know

Use your mediation skills when sticky situations pop up. For example, you may need to smooth ruffled feathers when a member of the wedding party has hurt feelings. Or, you can step in to solve a dispute between your Mom and the rehearsal dinner caterer. Be on the alert for ways you can calm things down, especially as you get closer to the wedding day.

‖‖

I didn't send wedding invitations to my coworkers, but they gave me an impromptu luncheon bridal shower this week, so am I obligated to invite them to the wedding after all?

No. Although an office shower is a delightful surprise, your coworkers have hosted this party knowing they weren't invited to the wedding. It's just a lovely show of support to a fellow employee.

People Problems

Who takes charge if a guest gets drunk during the reception?

Commission the best man and groomsmen ahead of time to discretely take care of the situation. It may be as simple as asking the guest to stop drinking and quiet down. Or, at the other extreme, it may be as complicated as arranging for the guest to be taken home, even if it means calling a taxi.

What if a guest is using drugs?

If you know that certain guests have used illegal drugs in the past, especially when partying, pass the word that this behavior is not welcome during your wedding reception. Then have a few reliable relatives or friends keep their eyes open during the reception, checking out the restrooms and any guests who seem to be disappearing from time to time. It's sad that you need to police your own party, but, as with an intoxicated guest, you are responsible to see to it that he or she doesn't drive.

What if the ceremony or reception sites are non-smoking venues, but you see a guest smoking?

Ask someone to speak to the smoker and mention that it is a non-smoking venue. Provide signs directing guests to a designated outdoor smoking area. Also, remove all ashtrays from the venue, which will give your guests a clue.

What happens if a guest grabs the microphone and tries to take over?

The guest doesn't have to be drunk to act out, but the same solution applies: best man or groomsmen to the rescue.

When choosing our attendants, how do we prevent hurt feelings?

The first rule of etiquette is that, just because you were asked to be an attendant at someone else's wedding, it doesn't require reciprocity. On the other hand, if you have more people than positions, try to include everyone you can in some way. For example, if the groom wants only three attendants, but has six really good friends, he can ask some of his friends to serve as ushers. Or, if the bride has an inordinate supply of little girls and teenagers who want to take part in her wedding, find *something* for each one to do. Young girls can serve as flower girls, bell ringers, or trainbearers. Teenage girls can serve as junior attendants, candle lighters, or gift table or guest book attendants. Young boys can serve as train bearers, pages, or bell ringers. Teenage boys can serve as junior attendants, ushers, or candle lighters. See Chapter 1 for job descriptions.

Don't choose your honor attendants until you've given your choice a lot of thought. You can avoid a mega-relationship problem by thinking before you speak. For example, when you become engaged, you may be so excited that you accidentally ask your best friend to be your maid of honor or best man, realizing later that your sister or brother should be your choice. So, take it slow when making these important decisions.

What happens if a member of your wedding party becomes ill and can't be at the wedding?

Rule number 1: don't panic. If your mother or one of the attendants comes down with the flu, for example, you have two choices: ask someone to fill in for that person, or don't worry about it. Perhaps one of your bridesmaids will fill in as your honor attendant, or one of your groomsmen will fill in as best man. If your mom or dad are incapacitated for some reason, that's heartbreaking, but the good news is this: at the end of the day, you'll still be a married couple, and your parent can experience your day via the photos and videos.

This is a second marriage for both of us. Are pre-wedding parties appropriate, such as an engagement party and bridal showers?

Of course! Not only are these parties appropriate, but you can establish gift registries as well, if you like.

How do I ask my dad not to bring his girlfriend to the wedding? (She's the woman who broke up my parents' marriage.)

Ask your Mom how she feels about it. If it doesn't bother her, let him bring her. However, if it bothers your Mom as much as it does you, have a talk with your dad. Explain to him that you want your wedding day to be as stress-free as possible, and that bringing his girlfriend may be awkward for everyone involved.

What do we do if our parents become control freaks?

This is an extra-sticky problem, especially if the controlling parent is paying for the entire wedding. Paying for the wedding doesn't give that person control of the wedding. This is *your* wedding and the decisions are up to you. I've seen brides' mothers who are so overbearing that the couple takes off and has a destination wedding, sans relatives of any kind. If a parent or relative wants to host a reception when they get back, fine. At least the crisis has been averted.

What if someone in our wedding party feels faint while standing during the ceremony?

I've been to so many weddings where someone collapses, which interrupts the ceremony, to say the least. Here are a few suggestions:

- Before the ceremony, place a chair at each end of the altar or huppah. If someone begins to feel faint, lead them to a chair and ask them to sit for the remainder of the ceremony.

- To prevent a problem in the first place, be sure everyone eats a little snack right before the ceremony, and during the ceremony do *not* lock your knees. Keep them bent slightly and discreetly alternate your weight from one foot to the other.

How do we handle relationship problems between family members?

It's unfortunate that a bride and groom have to wear kid gloves at their own wedding, but adults don't always act like grownups. For example, divorced parents can cause sparks to fly, so seat them several aisles apart during the ceremony and at separate tables during the reception. If a certain family member threatens to boycott your wedding if the "enemy" will be there, go ahead and send invitations to both of them and if one doesn't show up, it's not your problem. On the other hand, if your parents are divorced and your dad refuses to walk you down the aisle if your mom is there with her new squeeze, you do have a problem. In the case of a surly dad, ask your brother or someone else to walk you down the aisle. This is your party and if any guest, even one of your parents, acts like a selfish, immature brat, don't let it ruin your day.

My sister is my maid-of-honor and insists on going with me to shop for my wedding gown. However, she takes the fun out of it by nagging at me about my weight. She thinks I shouldn't shop until I've dropped a size. How do I handle this?

Easy answer: don't take her with you. Ask your mom or your best friend to go shopping with you. When you find the perfect gown, buy it. You can always have it altered if you lose weight between now and the wedding.

What if children are causing havoc at the reception?

Even though children may not be invited to your wedding, you can be sure several children will be on hand anyway. This can be a huge problem if small children are running around the reception venue, snatching olives off the buffet table and generally acting out. The solution to this problem is to anticipate it by setting aside a separate room or corner in which children can play, color, eat kiddie food, and watch videos. Of course, you'll need to provide a couple babysitters to ride herd. (Be sure they are sitters who are not involved in or are guests at your wedding.)

What's the best way to handle tension with the in-laws during the wedding planning?

If the groom feels uneasy around his future mother-in-law, or vice versa, one solution is to invite the mother to lunch—just the two of you: the groom with the bride's mother, or the bride with her groom's mother. Take her someplace nice, where the ambience is conducive to having a good talk. By "good talk," I mean saying things like, "Ashley and I really appreciate all your help with the wedding plans." Butter her up a little. Establish a genuine friendship, if you possibly can. The mother should appreciate your attention, and after your little one-on-one chat, tensions should ease considerably. This idea works for the fathers, too.

||||||||||||||||||||||||||||||||||||||||||||||||||||||||||||||||||||||||||||||||||||||||||||||||||||||||||||||

Etiquette 101

Never ask a guest for a gift receipt so that you can exchange the gift. Not only is it poor etiquette, but what if the guest is re-gifting to you?

||||||||||||||||||||||||||||||||||||||||||||||||||||||||||||||||||||||||||||||||||||||||||||||||||||||||||||||

What can I do when one of my attendants lets me down?

This is such a common problem: one of your attendants becomes totally irresponsible on your big day. For example, your best man doesn't follow through with his duties, even though he knows what they are. Or, friends and family members may let you down in a number of ways, so you need to face this possibility ahead of time and have a plan. Here it is: *love* and *tolerance*. In other words, try to be understanding while quietly delegating that person's responsibilities to someone else. Whatever you do, don't let immature, irresponsible friends ruin your wedding day. It's not worth it!

Index

About the Author

Diane Warner is the best-selling author of 23 books. She also writes for magazines and Websites, and is a popular speaker and radio and television guest. She has made more than 100 national radio and television appearances. She lives in Tucson, Arizona, with her author husband, Jack.

Books by Diane Warner

Published by Career Press:

Contemporary Guide to Wedding Ceremonies

Contemporary Guide to Wedding Etiquette

Complete Book of Wedding Vows, 2nd Edition

Complete Book of Wedding Toasts, 2nd Edition

Complete Book of Wedding Showers

Diane Warner's Wedding Question & Answer Book

Complete Book of Baby Showers

Diane Warner's Big Book of Parties

Diane Warner's Complete Book of Children's Parties

Diane Warner's Great Parties on Small Budgets

Best Wedding Ever

Published by F & W Publications, Betterway Books:

How to Have a Big Wedding on a Small Budget, 4th edition

Big Wedding on a Small Budget Planner and Organizer

How to Have a Fabulous, Romantic Honeymoon on a Budget

Beautiful Wedding Decorations and Gifts on a Small Budget

Picture-Perfect, Worry Free Weddings

How to Have a Great Retirement on a Limited Budget

to Have a Great Retirement on a Limited Budget

Published by John Wiley Publishing:

Single Parenting for Dummies, coauthored with Marion Peterson

Published by Pentan Overseas, Inc. (Books on Tape)

The Perfect Wedding Planner

Published by JISTWorks, Inc. (coauthored with her husband, Jack, and Clyde Bryan):

The Unauthorized Teacher's Survival Guide, 3rd Edition

The Inside Secrets of Finding a Teaching Job, 3rd Edition

Published by Accent Books, David C. Cook Publishing:

Puppets Help Teach

Puppet Scripts for Busy Teachers